Healing
is
Within
You

Learn from Your Past
Live in the Present
Love Your Future

CARLA CALDERAS

PRESS

Published by StoryBuilders Press

For information visit www.carlacalderas.com.

ISBN: 978-1-954521-75-9 - eBook

978-1-954521-76-6 - Paperback

979-8-89833-015-6 - Hardcover

Healing
is
Within
You

To my mom and my students—
your faith in me lit the way.

Table of Contents

Chapter One

Healing Is a Journey

Welcome to this new chapter of your life—the one where you are brave, committed, and ready to make a change. Maybe you are here because you don't know where to start, or maybe you have been on your healing journey for a while. Take a deep breath, put your hand on your heart, and know that we will do this together with love and patience.

Right now, you probably feel stuck—like your body keeps going through the motions from one day to the next. Weeks keep blurring together in a continuous cycle of wanting more and feeling disappointed when you don't see what you long for coming into your reality.

You are ready for a better life. One that allows you to go to bed feeling excited for the new day and the next set of opportunities for healing and growth, but it is difficult to know when or how to begin to make any lasting changes.

The sun rises and sets, and your mind tells you that another day has passed, filled with the same old things. Feeling trapped. Feeling like there's no escape to this cycle.

I understand. I have also felt overwhelmed, unsafe in my own body, and craving tranquility that at times felt impossible to obtain. After struggling for several years, I am here to give you hope and show you how you can get yourself out of that reality and into the one you truly deserve. I'm also here to support you while you begin to move freely with ease, compassion, and clarity into the life you are meant to have. I want you to see the next sunrise as a promise—reminding you that healing is within you, and you are capable of becoming the person you were born to be.

> *I want you to see the next sunrise as a promise—reminding you that healing is within you, and you are capable of becoming the person you were born to be.*

My heart is with you because getting unstuck is not easy. It will come with ups, downs, struggles, but also success, joy, and peace.

As a professional counselor and healing coach, I've worked with women like you and have seen so many transformations as clients worked with intention and commitment. As we embark on this adventure together, you will learn that we have more things in common than you may think and that many women face similar struggles. You will also learn more about my personal story and why my passion and mission in life is to heal and help others heal.

Maybe you have tried therapy, workshops, retreats, coaches, and healers, and deep down, you know all these have helped you feel better to some extent, but not fully. I want to remind you of what you may already know: True healing has to come from within. Doing "the work" can feel overwhelming, stressful, exhausting, and infuriating at times. We are all on a journey of self-discovery, healing, and growth, even though our paths may look a little different.

Perhaps you have done some inner work and have some self-awareness about where your behaviors and beliefs come from. Maybe you understand that the thoughts you have about yourself are hurtful and detrimental, and you notice doing to yourself what others have done to you in the past. Perhaps you are labeled as negative, judgmental, or a complainer. These words affect you and you don't really know what to do with this pain. So you push it down and pretend it's not there.

> *We are all on a journey of self-discovery, healing, and growth even though our paths may look a little different.*

You are doing the best you can at this moment, and you have no more emotional or mental capacity for more. You wonder if you don't make a change now, how to or if you can keep going.

You picked up this book because you are tired of feeling lonely or worthless and are looking for solutions. You are tired of feeling hopeless and without a clear purpose. You know there must be more to this sad, anxious, and hard life. You notice that you are not the only one suffering. Your family is suffering, your relationships are suffering, and your whole world is suffering. You have tried to "forget" about the difficult memories, attempting to be strong and push through, or maybe you have thought about ending it all.

Take a moment to consider your struggles. If you continue to escape, pretend you are okay, or choose to end it all, no healing can occur. If you stay on this avoidance path, you'll continue to lose yourself, your relationships, your job, or your health.

At times, you can see glimpses of your worth and the amazing things you deserve in life, but these moments seem to fade away. I am here to remind you that you are capable of lasting change, and all the answers are already inside you. I will show you how to connect back with your true self. You are meant to heal, and together we will get you to a place of harmony and connection.

I have been where you are, and I know that it is possible to embrace the beauty of ending each day with the certainty that you are one day closer to having a peaceful and joyful life.

Patience

I struggled with depression and anxiety during different moments in my life. Growing up with a single mom was difficult, and it affected me at different levels. It made me think that kids are a lot of work; you can either forget about them and choose a selfish life (like my dad who left us when I was just one year old), or you can forget about yourself and dedicate your life to your kids while you pretend not to appear depressed and overwhelmed, like my mom. In this journey, I have discovered understanding, forgiveness, but most of all, patience. Patience with myself and the people around me.

At one of my lowest points when I was fourteen years old, I took a box of pills and tried to end it all. Nothing happened to me physically, but back then, I made the decision that I was going to succeed in life so people would leave me alone. I decided I was going to have money so I wouldn't have to work two or three jobs like my mom. I decided I had to do it alone.

I was in for a big surprise, because in this healing journey, I have learned the importance of healthy friendships and a supportive community. You do not have to do it alone, and you deserve to be supported.

It takes time, compassion, and patience to heal. I know it may get uncomfortable, but I can tell you that this journey of healing from within will be worth it. I was also tired of feeling annoyed, angry, sad, and unsure if I should give up or keep going, being fueled by my trauma and lying to myself about wanting to be alone when in reality, I was craving connection, empathy, and love.

I read many inspirational books to find relief and hope. I went to therapy to understand my past. I looked into different religions for connection, but I still felt empty. All those avenues, paths, and resources gave me an incredible awareness. But actual healing happens when we consistently practice what we are learning and look for answers within.

As I got older, my life took many turns, but the core of my mission remained the same—to heal myself from all the trauma, pain, and sadness caused by growing up without a dad, being sexually abused, and being bullied.

I taught elementary school for a few years, where I saw suffering at a young age—from homelessness to molestation. Seeing this suffering opened my eyes to expand my life's mission to healing myself and helping others heal, because our world and our communities need healing. I got a master's degree in professional counseling, and as I write this, I have been a therapist for almost ten years, sitting with and serving hundreds of women like you and me—trapped in the darkness of sadness, trauma, and fears.

I write this book with love, hope, empathy, and passion. Love, because I believe in you, and I know you can find the love within you to heal. Hope that you give yourself the opportunity to apply the tools that my clients and I have used so you can live an amazing and fulfilling life. Empathy because I know the pain you are feeling and I know you are worthy of peace. Passion in my commitment to being here for you and being of service.

Empathy

We are all on different healing journeys. It's important to have empathy and compassion for ourselves and others, because we don't know the journeys others have been on just by looking at them.

To give you some context and examples, I want to introduce you to Victoria, Nancy, and Gaby. These aren't their real names, and not every element of their stories are exactly factual. As you read about them, they feel real because their lives are based on a merging of women I've met with and counseled over my years in the profession.

Each of these women has parts of their lives that are going well and challenges they face. These women may remind you of someone you know or of yourself. You may be triggered as you look at what is missing from your life by comparing it to theirs. You may be surprised to notice that the things you don't like about them are actually things you don't like about yourself.

No matter whom they remind you of, I invite you to find room for forgiveness, acceptance, and compassion. Learning about these women and their growth can be a window of what is possible for you.

As you read on, you are going to learn about their lives, their strengths, their struggles, and their successes. By building empathy, you can apply their lessons to improve your own life. My hope is that the stories of Victoria, Nancy, and Gaby inspire you and give you confidence in your healing journey. I invite you to learn from them and see how they have applied the strategies we are going to explore.

Victoria

Victoria wakes up exhausted in her large but lonely apartment downtown. She feels annoyed about having to interact with people today. The first decision to make after her shower is which outfit to wear. To feel powerful and win the case today, she wonders if she should wear the black Versace dress or the tan tweed Chanel suit.

As she puts on her makeup, she notices the *eleven lines* deepening between her eyebrows and wonders if she should start getting injectables. She rushes to finish getting ready and gets angry when she realizes that she does not have time to make her coffee, so she drives to the coffee shop a few blocks away from her luxury apartment building.

Victoria is the type of woman who believes that speed limits are suggestions because no one is going to tell her what to do or how to do it. At the drive-through, she feels frustrated about people being too slow and taking too long to order. If you saw her driving her luxurious Mercedes-Benz, you would think she is an angry, stressed, and heartless woman. At the same time, you may also envy her or want to be like her as she seems so confident and unstoppable.

Looking at her, you would never know that she was neglected as a child. She grew up with an emotionally unavailable single mom. Her mom waited tables and was committed to finding the love of her life, which meant Victoria was never a priority. Victoria learned to fend for herself, and since no parental figure seemed interested in her, she learned not to be interested in others.

After many years of feeling irritated and resentful, she began reading self-help books. She realized that no matter how much money and material things she accumulates, she doesn't seem to feel fulfilled or satisfied by them. Now she's been promoted for her willingness and attitude to "win at all costs," and she is busier than ever. Inside she feels furious, lonely, and desperate. She wonders why she has not found a partner and why she does not seem to have many friends around.

Nancy

Nancy lives with her husband in the far suburbs of a major city. She never had any children of her own but has been a stepmom for eight years to her husband's two kids from a previous marriage. They are now in high school, and Nancy works tirelessly to feel accepted by them.

She has been a teacher since she graduated college. Seeing "her kids" is one of the only things that brings her happiness these days. She is excellent at her job and is loved by her students and their parents. Nancy is busy. When she is not planning her lessons, she is reading or walking her dog. The hardest parts of Nancy's days start at dinnertime as she tries to connect with her apathetic husband.

She struggles to fall asleep due to constant thoughts about her life: wondering if she is happy, wondering if she wants to stay in this marriage, and wondering what else she can add to her to-do list to find a sense of connection and happiness. After this rumination, she looks at her sleeping husband next to her and realizes that she feels lonely and empty.

The loneliness and lack of sleep, coupled with the chronic busyness she uses to fill the void, are causing her mental and physical health to suffer.

Gaby

As Gaby cries on her couch, she feels lost, overwhelmed, and so alone that she has considered suicide, but the guilt of leaving her kids without a mother stops her from attempting it. She recently realized that by giving herself and her life to her children and husband, she has forgotten about herself.

She lives in a small house on the city outskirts. She is married with three children: two teens and a later-in-life child. She is a dedicated mother who lives for her family.

You can typically find her at her children's school volunteering, taking her kids to multiple after-school activities, or at the grocery store buying the supplies necessary to host her next church gathering while keeping her busy family of five fed and the household running smoothly.

Fighting through the traffic of the city and dealing with the disconnected people on the sidewalk and in the shops makes her feel sad and hopeless. Most days, she finds herself staring straight ahead as she drives or walks, avoiding eye contact with those around her.

She grew up believing in the importance of serving others first. As an overachieving giver, she is constantly pouring her love and energy into others. When she thinks about doing something for herself, she feels guilty. Once she drops her kids off at school, she goes home to a quiet house where she can finally take the mask off and stop pretending that she has it all together.

Hope

Now let's look within if you see parts of yourself in Victoria: You may wonder why no matter how much you achieve, it feels like it's never enough, and you want to have meaningful relationships, but they also feel like a waste of time. What about feeling worried, focusing on all the what-ifs and what could go wrong in your life? Perhaps you identify with Nancy. If you wake up most days feeling sad, numb, and guilty for feeling depressed, you possibly resonate with Gaby.

For various reasons, somewhere along the way, all three women had forgotten who they really were at their core, and instead, they developed layers of protection or numbing habits. These layers appear to be protecting them from more pain, but in reality, these habits are hurting them by preventing them from being vulnerable and creating healthy relationships with others and with themselves.

Let's be honest. You are tired of feeling worried and hurt, like the world is against you, and like you are alone and no one cares. You know that this pain is getting to you, and it is affecting you more than you want to admit. It seems easier to look at others and judge them because you struggle to look within and accept that you don't like this version of yourself.

I am writing this book because I want to be here for you and guide you into a beautiful new life. As you will see from observing our three friends' progress and change, everyone is capable of making lasting changes as long as they develop awareness, choose intentionally, and have the unwavering hope that healing is possible.

Our stories are important, and we will get to yours shortly. For now, think about each of these women you just met. Was it uncomfortable for you, reading about these women who are not fulfilled and just seem to go through the motions in their life? Do you identify with any of them? Or do you know someone like them?

What would you think about Victoria? That she is arrogant, closed off, and selfish—or powerful and wealthy? And Nancy? Do you wonder what is wrong with her, or do you know exactly how she feels because you can feel the same anxiety crawling into your body as you read about her? What about Gaby? She doesn't have to work and seems like the perfect mom, so why does she seem so sad if she has it all?

Victoria, Nancy, and Gaby will be our guides for this journey of healing. I used my personal and professional experience to create them so that I can give you plenty of examples as we do this work together. I will also be sharing more about my past and my struggles because I want to give you hope. Because with time and conscious effort, you can heal. There is light at the end of the tunnel. No matter what you have been through, you are worthy of feeling better and healing.

I can tell you with confidence that there is peace in my heart. Most of my days are good, but I also have amazing days and also not-so-good days. The difference is that I now know what to do to get myself back on track. I will show you how too. During this journey together, I will share stories, tools, and strategies to help you become the happy, beautiful, worthy person you are at your core.

You felt called to pick up this book because you want to feel better, you want to feel happy, and you are hopeful that healing is possible. I'm glad! Now is a great time to begin your best life. The good news is, the answers you are looking for are already inside you, waiting to be found.

During our time together in this book, you will work to explore your past, implement tools to help you in your day-to-day life, and create a future that inspires you.

The journey ahead will be uncomfortable and incredibly rewarding. You are worthy of it! You are stronger than you think, and deep down, you know, you deserve to be happy.

Here is what you can expect as we move forward:

The Past

I will guide you through exploring your past with compassion. Maybe you have tried to suppress the discomfort and pain you have been through, or maybe you have tried to put the struggles and trauma in a box and bury it. In order for us to move forward, we have to look at where you come from so that we know where we are going. You'll learn how to find answers to questions such as the following:

"What has happened to me that has marked me?"

"How is my past affecting me today?"

"How can I grow from it?'

When you can release the urge to ignore and avoid your circumstances and what you have experienced, you will find yourself on the other side feeling stronger, more confident, and more at peace. You'll strengthen your resilience and perseverance and find a deeper sense of courage as you navigate the rest of your life.

The Present

Once you allow yourself to explore your past, it's time to take action. In part 2, you will gain an understanding of how your thoughts, feelings, and behaviors are interconnected. You'll see the unique perspectives of Victoria, Nancy, and Gaby as they take steps to make lasting changes that will prepare them for the amazing future they deserve.

I will provide you with the tools and the space to incorporate changes that feel achievable. We will look at making healthy changes and aligning your thoughts and behaviors to create the reality that you want. Small changes are what can create remarkable progress in the long run. Understanding how your thoughts and behaviors influence how you feel will be a game changer.

The Future

When you have clarity on where you're going, the path ahead opens up and things flow. In part 3, you'll allow yourself to see a brighter future with tools to help you visualize, believe, and receive the gift of a healed life.

You will take the time to identify what you want your life to look like, visualize it, and create steps that will help you get there. We will also take a look at Victoria, Nancy, and Gaby to see how they have used the tools described to live a life that lights them up.

After reading this book, you will feel inspired, committed, and ready to live an amazing life! You will feel proud of yourself for taking the time to work on yourself. You will also notice that by working on yourself and improving the relationship with yourself, your relationships with others also improve.

While I can't sit across from you over coffee as a friend, or sit with you in my office as a client, we will take this journey together. I will guide you to discover that what happened to you in the past is impacting your present and limiting your future, but it doesn't have to be that way.

As you gain access to the sunshine you have dimmed inside you, you will discover that your power is in the present and there are things you can do to influence your future. There is hope, and I will show you the possibilities.

Let's get started! I am excited for you to discover how your past is part of you and can be your strength. May you discover that healing is within you!

First, I have a request from you. Think of it as coming not from me but from your higher self, the best version of yourself, or your healed self. Give yourself the time, patience, and compassion to go on this journey. Allow yourself twenty to thirty minutes per day to read this book, journal about it, and do the exercises we will do here together.

Find a quiet place and a time where you can be alone. Allow yourself to feel and release the emotions that you have kept stored for a long time. This book can be the first step you take toward your healing journey, or it can be the next one you take. What I can guarantee is that it won't be the last. Healing is a journey. Let's begin.

Another Day

As the days pass
I think about my life
I sit around and wait
For the spark in my veins

I work, I pray, I plan in dismay
I pretend to be happy and hope not to get caught
Filled with doubt and emptiness,
More things were bought

The memories mean nothing
Time is an illusion
No one is here
Is this my conclusion?

Today is my birthday
I feel sad and inept
I'm confused and in pain
Because this I can't accept

Someone please help me
I'm crying for aid
Is that even possible?
Or do I just need to help myself?

I don't know what I want
Can I even be happy?
But how do I get there
When the climb seems so rocky

God, are you there?
I'm tired of this stress
Can you please help me?
I'm becoming depressed

I guess I will wait
Not sure for how long
My body is exhausted
And my soul is losing hope.

—Carla Calderas

I had a few years of feeling sad around my birthday in my early thirties. I was feeling lonely, hopeless, and frustrated for feeling this way. I felt tired of masking the pain and pretending to be okay in front of others. Writing this poem was my way of releasing my emotions and allowing myself to feel and cry.

PART ONE

The Past

Chapter Two

The Only Way Out Is Through

Victoria was glad it was a work-from-home day when her alarm went off to start the morning. It was nice to have a day to work outside of the law firm once a week. She'd already planned to spend most of her time working on her opening statements for the big celebrity custody battle that would begin in court the following week.

Those familiar thoughts popped into her mind as she brushed her teeth.

Life is hard, but I've learned how to fight back.

I am the hero who saves herself. I don't sit around waiting to be rescued.

I create my own destiny.

Failure is not an option, and victory is mine to claim.

Don't think I can do it? Watch me.

For a second, her heart softened as she tapped into the reason why she loves her job—helping children. She understood that she was part of something bigger than herself.

I'm looking out for the kids stuck in the middle of two adults and all their drama.

She always felt lighter when she thought about the way she advocated for the kids who were too young to speak for themselves.

She remembered being five years old, walking home from school, wondering most days if today would be the day that her mom would pick her up, give her a hug, and talk about their day. Every so often, she'd even gather enough courage to think about asking her to play with her, but tears and disappointment was what she experienced as her mom said no and she was left alone. She never met her dad, and after asking if she'd get to meet him, her mom made it clear that he wanted nothing to do with her.

When Victoria cried, her mom got mad. It was easier just to be tough, not a playful, all-smiles girl she saw in school or on TV. She was more like a little adult than a child. Finding food around the house to make her own meals and getting herself up and ready for school helped her become fiercely independent.

She used to walk past her mom's open bedroom door and tried not to look inside as her mom did things in her bed with her boyfriends. When she was seven, her mom's latest boyfriend came into her bedroom and locked the door behind him. Her mom was at work, and Victoria didn't understand what was happening to her. This continued to happen until her mom found someone else who made more money.

It wasn't until she was a teenager and her friends were talking about losing their virginity that she realized that her virginity was taken from her. She tried her best to ignore her thoughts when they popped up, deciding that it didn't matter and the best thing to do was leave the past in the past. She decided that she was now in charge of her body, and she was going to do whatever it took to look good and sleep with as many men and women as possible as this gave her a sense of control.

Before leaving for college, she finally decided to tell her mom about the multiple times she was raped, and her mom shook it off, saying things like, "No, I don't think so. Why are you making this up? If you're trying to get attention, you're going about it the wrong way. If this really happened, you probably asked for it."

They never talked about it again. She didn't go to counseling or receive any support. Instead, she did her best to pretend like it never happened.

Why am I thinking about this now? It only makes me angry.

With a shake of her head, she tried to focus on her makeup, adding the finishing touches before she left for the coffee shop.

Nodding to herself in the mirror, Victoria thought, *I look good today. Ha! I always do.* Her physical appearance was one of the only things that made her smile. *This, right here, is why I don't have many female friends.*

They were jealous of her good looks and the fact that she could have any man she wanted. But she didn't need a man in her life; she was independent. She could afford anything she wanted, so a man was not needed.

At the coffee shop, she placed her order and got to work at a table in the corner, seated in a way that she could scan the entire room from time to time to feel safe. When they called her name to pick up her iced skinny latte, she jumped, almost knocking her laptop to the floor. Her eyes quickly scanned the room once again to make sure no one saw her embarrassing reaction. Victoria threw her shoulders back and walked confidently to the counter. Occasionally sipping on her latte, she created an incredible opening argument. It was just the right blend of facts and coldhearted wit that she was known for in the courtroom.

I am a badass! I deserve a fucking shopping trip on the way home.

Victoria was going to debut her latest power suit next week, so on the way home, she decided to grab herself a new designer handbag and some shoes too.

Why not? I work hard, and I deserve all this!

All the compliments she received at the high-end stores made her feel proud and worthy, but only for a few minutes. Trying on the new shoes and handbag and thinking about the suit at home, she knew she'd be an intimidating force in the courtroom.

By the time she got home with the new purchases, her mind was racing with other thoughts. She added the shoebox to the pile of boxes in her spacious closet and set the bag on its new shelf. The thrill was over.

Why am I always so angry?

The thought left her mind as quickly as it came, and Victoria heard the familiar sound of her email notifications going off where she had set her phone down in her living room.

Processing

Your past plays a part in who you become as an adult. Over time, you create automatic habits and subconscious ways of doing things that may seem like part of your personality. Maybe you learned to hide and push your feelings down, all to get a false sense of safety. That has served a purpose, but now it may not align with the person you are meant to become. When you can identify patterns and behaviors that no longer serve you, you'll begin an incredible journey of healing. Processing our feelings is part of a healed life and the only way we find true peace.

The only way out is through, so understanding your origin and its impact is necessary to improve your self-awareness and learn that your behaviors are sometimes reactions to the experiences in your past. You will also obtain clarity about who you are and learn how to avoid repeating the same patterns. Working through your past also brings you one step closer to having the life you want for yourself. You deserve to step into the best version of yourself, and it starts with reminding yourself that you're worthy of doing the work to get there. You won't break; you will actually find tranquility and lightness.

Here, you'll learn about the ways your past can keep you feeling trapped in a cycle that affects your present. Then we'll look at some of the best ways for you to realize that healing is within you by opening yourself up to processing your past and learning from it to then take charge of your present. Once you have that understanding, lasting change can take place. This may be uncomfortable because of trauma. Be patient and take time to cry or scream if you feel the need.

Gratitude

Your past has gotten you to where you are today, so in some ways, it deserves gratitude because it has gotten you here. Maybe you are financially stable, have a good husband, or have a great career. In some ways, it has worked for you. But in other ways, you know that something is missing. True and lasting healing is what you're looking for. The problem is, you've learned ways to handle the past without actually working through the pain. Consider the following ways people who have experienced a traumatic past or painful moments avoid processing their pain.

"Just move on. Let it go. It's over, and there's nothing I can do about it."

I acknowledge that sometimes part of you may want to leave the past in the past—things that were hurtful, traumatic, profoundly sad, or mixed with other emotions you want to create distance from. Unfortunately, by attempting to leave them behind and forget about them, they stay with you, hurt you, and affect your body and your outlook on life. You may have experienced this firsthand. Deep down, you feel like a ticking bomb that can explode any second.

How long have you noticed yourself living the same patterns of behavior or having similar issues pop up in your life? These unhealed experiences and events can start to affect your daily life slowly until you don't recognize yourself anymore. You may think it's just your personality, or you try to convince yourself: "I'm just having a bad day/month/ year. . ."

But when you don't allow yourself to address and release those emotions, they show up whether you want them to or not. Have you ever tried to hold a beach ball under the water? Trying to bury your emotions is a similar experience. I've seen the effects in my clients, and you may see them in yourself too. Here are just a few of the ways your unresolved past can find its way into your daily life:

- Impatience with strangers
- Judging others

- Envying others for what they have
- Feeling constant tension and worry
- Feeling like you are trapped and there's no way out
- Running around feeling busy and heading nowhere
- Lack of motivation
- Feeling like you don't have a purpose
- Trying to relax with a massage and feeling the tension as soon as you leave the spa
- Living with constant pressure and little hope

"The world is awful, so why bother trying?"

Like Victoria, when you experience trauma in your life, it can be difficult to understand why it happened. It can also create a chain reaction of feeling angry, guilty, and ashamed. It can also create stages of distancing yourself from others, questioning your worth, and dimming your light.

When life has felt unfair over and over again, it's easy to believe that the world is against you. That no matter what you do, things will never change. When you've been rejected, dismissed, or left to figure things out alone, it makes sense to feel that way.

You start living in a space of anxiety and fear, always waiting for something to go wrong. You walk through life feeling angry, overwhelmed, and exhausted. You look at people and expect the worst. You question if anyone is really on your side. It feels like the whole world is pushing back against you, like nothing comes easily.

At some point, this mindset can wear you down. It's exhausting to always be on guard, feeling like you have to fight through each day. You reach a point where you just want to stop trying because, really, what is the point if you'll continuously face negative situations?

By not allowing yourself to heal from your experiences, you will continue to feel like everyone and everything around you is working together to keep you stuck.

As you face new challenges and setbacks, you may find yourself nodding along and thinking, "Of course, this is how it would go for me. Nothing good ever happens to me."

But those thoughts can be transformed. Now is the time to start processing your past.

Transformation

Trauma is part of everyone's human experience. It isn't just the big, obvious moments—the things we see in movies or hear about in extreme cases. It's not just loss, death, or violence. Yes, those are traumas, but so are the smaller, quieter moments that changed something in you. The experiences that made you question yourself, made you feel unsafe, or made you put on a mask just to get through the day. Maybe it was growing up in poverty, your parents divorcing, or a best friend moving away at the exact moment you needed them the most. Trauma is anything that shifts you. It made you start acting out of fear instead of trust or made you feel like you had to be a different version of yourself to be okay or survive.

At some point, every single one of us will go through sadness, loss, or heartache. It's unavoidable. But what if these difficulties weren't just moments of random suffering? What if they were shaping you into the person you need to become? What if they were giving you the ability to connect with others in a deeper way? When you're in the middle of it, that thought can feel impossible. When you do the work to heal, you may realize that the hardest moments were actually creating something in you rather than shutting you down.

> *When you do the work to heal, you may realize that the hardest moments were actually creating something in you rather than shutting you down.*

That is transformation—going from being a victim, wounded, and hurt to this empowered, confident, and unshakable person. You are not the things that happen to you. Your past is part of your story, but it doesn't get to define who you are.

Instead of living in a space where things happened to you and now you are powerless, what if you shifted to seeing it as happening for you? Instead of staying stuck in the pain, allowing yourself to ask, "What is this teaching me? How is this making me stronger?" can change everything.

Please understand, I know this process isn't easy. I also felt like dying and embraced by anger. We all have low points in our life; they are part of the journey.

I want to introduce you to one of my favorite authors, Og Mandino. His story reminds me that transformation is possible, even from the lowest places. There was a time in his life when he was battling deep sadness, numbing his pain with alcohol and struggling with suicidal thoughts. He was at a point where it felt like there was no way out. But then, something shifted. He walked into a library and started reading inspirational books. That one small choice in a quiet moment of hope led him to completely transforming his life. Og didn't just find healing. He became a voice of encouragement for millions of others. He went on to write many inspirational books, including *The Greatest Salesman in the World.* His journey is such a powerful example of how our lowest points don't have to be the end of our story. They can become the beginning of something meaningful and beautiful.

As you start looking at your past, you might come up against feelings of shame, guilt, or even regret. You might blame yourself for the way things turned out. The truth is, you were doing the best you could with what you knew at the time. You were surviving. Now you are becoming aware that you have the power within you to transform. Transformation is about embracing who you truly are and who you were before the trauma.

As you continue to transform, I want to invite you to own your full story—not just the painful parts, but also the moments of love, joy, and hope. Sometimes we focus on what hasn't gone well and minimize the good times because there are few or they don't seem as big. Healing is as real as trauma, and you are on your way to a healed life. Happiness is a part of life just as much as challenges. Give yourself the opportunity to embrace it all.

Meaning

When we are healing, one of the tools to move through our past is to find meaning. Consider looking at our pain to find the lesson or learning experience from the event. When we look back with curiosity and ask "What can I learn from this?" we give ourselves the gift of hope—hope that there is opportunity for growth. With hope, we can continue our healing journey with purpose and intention.

The story of Viktor Frankl, a psychiatrist who survived the horrors of the Nazi concentration camps, comes to mind. He witnessed unimaginable suffering and cruelty, not just to those around him, but also to himself. He lost his family, his freedom—everything.

But in the middle of that darkness, what helped him survive wasn't physical strength—it was meaning. He held on to the belief that his suffering wasn't pointless. He told himself that if he could endure the pain, he might use his experience to help others one day. Then he did.

After the war, he wrote *Man's Search for Meaning* and helped millions of people understand that even in our lowest moments, we can choose to create purpose. That has stayed with me. Because when we can give meaning to our pain and believe that what we're going through can help someone else, it becomes more than our hurting. It becomes part of our healing.

An event can occur, something can happen to me, and I have a choice to find the meaning that can help me keep going. I can see the situation as "It is happening *to* me" or as "It is happening *for* me."

The difference is, do I want to be a victim or be empowered by the situation? You can choose to see it as a learning experience and something you can grow from. I invite you to change your perspective on what has happened to you. Trust that it happened *for* you, to make you a stronger and more resilient person. It can be the experience that connects you to others and what helps you heal our world. It's never too late to make a decision to learn more about yourself and the ways your past has shaped you.

I want to tell you a story on how finding meaning helped me transform—from feeling devastated and unworthy to understanding with compassion and feeling worthy. I can still remember how my feelings changed from happiness and pride to confusion and pain when I showed my mom the score on a test from my third-grade class. I felt like I did a great job. I was proud to pull out the paper with a big "80%"

written at the top and hold it out for her to see. But when she told me it wasn't good enough, my heart sank.

At that moment as a third-grader, I felt like she was telling me I wasn't good enough. I spent decades trying to work diligently to erase that feeling. I was getting the 100 percents, excelling in school, proving to myself that I was intelligent and that I could meet or exceed the expectations placed on me. On the outside, I was doing everything I thought I was supposed to do—getting the grades, performing, achieving.

But at what cost?

Inside, I felt like I still wasn't good enough. I was carrying this pressure, this need to keep up an image of success, and it was exhausting. I was frustrated, overwhelmed, and constantly pushing, never allowing myself to just be.

The stress wasn't just in my mind; it was in my body. I had tension headaches that followed me through most of my teens and twenties. I would get stress hives with big tests or academic pressure. I couldn't sleep well. Even in my sleep, my body held on to the pressure. I would wake up with impressions of my fingernails dug into my palms. I wake up the same way from time to time even now, my body still remembering the old pattern of holding everything in, bracing for something that isn't there anymore.

That's why I am honest about healing. We are constantly healing. We are going to face triggers, hints of the past, and reminders of what we have been through. In this healing journey, it isn't about being done with healing; it's about embracing the journey. Instead of seeing the reminders as proof that we haven't healed, we can see them as reminders of how far we've come.

When we feel like we're not good enough, when we believe we have to keep proving ourselves, it comes at a cost. We move through life without really enjoying it. We keep going, keep pushing, but inside, we're exhausted. We tell ourselves that once we accomplish the next thing, we'll feel like we're enough. But the finish line just keeps moving, and it seems like we can never reach it.

As I applied the tool of finding meaning, I realized that I am always

> *In this healing journey, it isn't about being done with healing; it's about embracing the journey. Instead of seeing the reminders as proof that we haven't healed, we can see them as reminders of how far we've come.*

good enough, and the excitement and pride I felt right before I showed my mom the test is our natural state. Sometimes when we encounter challenges, we hide and forget who we truly are. Part of finding healing within you is going back to your true self and who you were before the pain. It is possible to look within and live in harmony with your body, your thoughts, and who you are at your core.

As I applied the tool of finding meaning to my third-grade example, I realized something important. My mother wasn't telling me I wasn't good enough. The meaning I discovered was that she was trying to say, in her own way, "You are capable of more. I believe in you."

> *Part of finding healing within you is going back to your true self and who you were before the pain.*

That shift didn't happen overnight. It took some evolving on my part. I put in the emotional work by accepting what happened, making space for the pain, and then choosing to see it a different way. Thanks to one of my psychology classes, I began to understand that her words weren't meant to harm me, even though they did. They came from a place of wanting to see me thrive.

With this awareness, I can now listen to myself and my body when I've done enough, and I can allow myself a time to rest. I remind myself that I am safe, I am strong, and good things are on their way. As humans, we are always transforming. There is power in choosing the meaning that helps us grow.

Acceptance

Accepting what happened does not mean it was okay or that you agree with it. It means that you realize that it did happen. It is part of you and your story, and it doesn't have to define you. Accepting what happened to us is uncomfortable, and I want you to know that without discomfort, there is no growth. Once you accept this, we can continue to move forward. What I ask of you is to stay present and be kind to yourself as this is a necessary step we have to take to heal. Let's start with Victoria.

The sexual abuse she experienced as a child didn't go away when she realized her mom didn't want to discuss it. It stayed with her on a subconscious level until she made the conscious choice to address it and work through it. Getting the right outfits, having a strict exercise routine, and controlling her food intake became some of her top priorities so that she could feel some sense of control due to living in a chaotic and unpredictable environment.

She struggled with maintaining female friends in her life because they were uncomfortable with the way she sought out male attention, but she'd tell herself it was probably because they were jealous of her. She'd tell herself she didn't really care if she had friends because they just slowed her down.

She put herself through college by waiting tables like her mom, applying for all the scholarships she could find, and taking out student loans. When she studied on her laptop in her favorite coffee shop, it was hard to be present when she was thinking about a million other things she could be doing besides classwork to make more money.

Closed off, stressed out, and being able to tear people to shreds with her strong and demanding personality, she was never the kind of woman to be mistaken for someone who was considered softhearted. Victoria preferred to be seen as strong, driven, and intelligent.

On some level, creating her tough, no-nonsense, emotionally detached personality made her feel like she was in charge of her life. Her strict food monitoring and exercise routines kept her feeling tough and able to physically protect herself.

After a few years of working with her therapist, she began to see that her life was not really working for her. She accepted that her trauma caused her to develop shields because she never felt safe. She could not remember the last time she felt joy or peace; she wasn't even sure if she had ever felt that. Victoria learned that by trying to avoid becoming her mom, she had started repeating the same patterns with her relationships as men came and went. She understood that while others called her a "bitch," she was just reacting to her unprocessed trauma and protecting herself. She accepted that she experienced a lot of trauma and uncertainty, and it was now time to heal and welcome a better life.

Another benefit of looking at her past was that she understood why she loved helping children. She actually had a huge heart for kids who got caught up in their parents' divorce wars. Part of her wanted to heal as she was helping these children find healthy and happy homes. Addressing her past with the help of her therapist helped Victoria begin to heal. She was now better equipped to identify her triggers and manage her life in healthier ways.

Awareness

Victoria is beginning to see herself more clearly. She's been moving through life with this tough exterior, convinced that she has to keep up a persona of having it all together because she felt broken and rejected. For so long, she believed that if she allowed people to get close to her, they would see right through to her. They'd realize she's not as strong as she seems, that she's somehow a fraud.

With her new awareness, she's recognizing that this pattern of behavior isn't serving her. She's realizing that her fear of being truly seen is keeping her from building deep, meaningful relationships. She has developed the awareness that she had been rejecting herself by not allowing deep friendships to form. Now that she sees it, she has a choice. She can start making changes that help her open up, trust, and let people in.

In her relationships, she's also becoming aware of something big. She had always wanted to feel in control—especially when it came to dating—but that need for control had been pushing away the healthy, secure partnerships she truly wanted. She's starting to see that by trying to protect herself, she had actually been keeping good men at a distance. But now, she's shifting. She's reminding herself that it's okay to let go. That she can trust herself to choose the right person. She's learning to listen to that gut feeling telling her when something feels safe and good and when it's time to lean in instead of pulling away. She's creating the awareness that self-love, self-acceptance, and self-forgiveness are the path to follow for her healing.

Victoria never wanted to be seen as weak—she wanted to be known as strong. But when she steps back and looks at the moments that make her feel most like herself, they aren't the moments of being untouchable or tough. They are the moments when she's connecting with kids in court, when she sees their trust in her, and when she knows she's making a difference. That's when she feels alive.

With this awareness, she's starting to understand that kindness isn't weakness. It's part of who she is. She doesn't have to hide it. She doesn't have to hold back. She can embrace it fully—because when she does, she feels accepted, fulfilled, and like she belongs.

Creating awareness is also possible for you. I invite you to take some time to look back and see what has worked in your life and what hasn't. Just like Victoria, you have the power to notice the patterns, both the ones that have served you and the ones that haven't.

This kind of self-reflection isn't about blame or shame. It's about compassion, curiosity, and honesty. When you can see things clearly, you can start to make different choices. You can choose to let go of old beliefs that no longer fit and step into a version of yourself that feels more true to who you are. Awareness is the first step toward change. When you practice it with love, grace, and courage, it becomes the foundation for your healing and growth.

Let's Reflect

Do you see how now is the perfect time to look at your past? There are gems to discover by creating meaning and awareness. Let's get started!

While working on the following exercises, I encourage you to look at your past as candidly as possible. This isn't a time to judge yourself or compare your experiences to someone else's. Trust that what comes up is exactly what you need to look into and release.

Allow yourself some quiet time with your journal. Ask yourself the following questions.

Explore:

- Which events from my past do I continue to think about and want to forget?
- Are there patterns that keep repeating themselves, or am I reliving the same event with different people?
- What events from my past still feel heavy in my heart?
- What within me is still asking to be seen, softened, and healed?

Learn:

- Is there a lesson here for me to learn?
- What meaning can I find in that experience?
- What do I need to forgive myself for?
- What can I learn from this situation?

Shift:

- What behavior changes can I implement to break this pattern?
- What mindset changes would be healthier for me to create a different reality for myself?
- How is my life going to change once I begin to accept my past with compassion instead of resistance?

I know looking back can feel heavy, but healing occurs when we gently look at what we have been working so hard to hide. Processing creates healing. We transform by finding meaning and gratitude in our experiences. We create awareness so that the patterns don't keep repeating. You deserve to heal!

Chapter Three

The Influence of the Past

Nancy woke up before the alarm again, putting one hand on her tight chest while the other one turned the alarm off. Her husband didn't react to her movements as he slept peacefully.

My husband of eight years. The man I fell for head over heels, accepting that he was divorced and coparenting two kids when we met. I wonder if we'll be able to get that head-over-heels-in-love feeling back anytime soon.

She felt the familiar tightness in her chest spreading around her throat, choking her.

Tiptoeing across the plush carpet and into the bathroom, Nancy slid the pocket door shut before she began gasping for breath.

No, no, no . . . I'm okay. Just slow down. Breathe.

She flattened her hands against the countertop, staring blankly into the sink through glossy eyes. She tried to imagine an invisible hand loosening its grip around her throat and chest as she breathed in and out, in and out.

It was time to get ready for school. Splashing water on her face and watching it wash her tears away, she took one last big breath, lifted her head, and thought about the presentations "her kids" were doing today. She was excited to see their little smiling faces, and she mentally went through her class list, thinking about the perfect morning greeting each one would need as they walked into her classroom. Some would want their secret handshakes, while others would need a hug and a "You've got this!" from her.

Funny, she realized, she always just called it "school" instead of "work." Teaching elementary school kids was more fun than work for her. Unless it was an evaluation day.

Having the administrator walking around her room with her tablet, made her so dizzy she felt like her soul was trying to escape her body through the top of her head. Two of her more empathetic students would notice her shaky hands and would do their best to show the principal that they were learning a lot in her class. Her evaluations were always good. Deep down, she knew they would be, but she just couldn't get those thoughts out of her mind.

This is the day she'll finally see that I'm a fraud. Then I'll be fired and lose the only good thing in my life.

She'd immediately think about her mom and shame herself for so carelessly dismissing that there was at least one other good thing in her life.

On her way to school, Nancy called her mom for their morning chat. This was part of their routine since her first day as a teacher, fourteen years ago. Her mom asked about the presentations and had Nancy remind her which students had which topics, who was nervous, and who volunteered to go first.

As they chatted while she drove, Nancy could feel the morning's tension easing away. On her way home, she'd call her again to recap the day and talk about the snacks she would gather together for her two stepchildren and their friends for their first Friday movie night. She knew that her mom always had the best advice.

Nancy's mom used to host Friday movie nights for her and her friends just about every week when she was in high school. To prepare, her mom would send her stepfather to the grocery store with a list, and the two of them would decorate the basement in a way that matched the movie, whether it was a theme or a particular scene they loved. It was silly and over-the-top, but they loved spending time together. Her friends all loved Nancy's mom too. It wasn't out of the ordinary for her to pop in and out of the room, replenishing snacks or even sitting with them to watch one of her favorite scenes with them.

Her mom truly was her best friend back then, and still was today. Thinking back on those times always made her smile. But her smile vanished as she thought about the Friday movie night she was about to host in her own home.

The tightness began to make its way back across her chest. The closer she got to her house, the more her brain felt like it was too big for her skull.

It has to be perfect. This could be the moment they start to love you as their stepmom.

Even as she thought it, she doubted she could pull off such a feat. It was always so easy between Nancy and her mom. Maybe it was because they were together her whole life. These kids met her when she was twenty-eight and she married their forty-three-year-old dad. She stopped keeping track of the ratio of eyerolls to smiles from them—eyerolls were winning by a landslide.

After dinner, her stepson claimed the home theater for his friends, and her stepdaughter took out some blankets for her friends to use in the living room. Nancy began making microwave popcorn as she organized candy baskets for each room. As their guests arrived and went to their areas with her stepchildren, the scent of her made-from-scratch chocolate chip cookies filled the air. She breathed in the familiar memory of making the same cookies with her mom and felt her stomach flip as she thought that maybe, someday, she could make them with her stepchildren.

Nancy slowly and optimistically made her way into the home theater with the first plateful.

"Who wants cookies?"

Her stepson jumped up as his friends quietly watched him snatch the plate from her hands and grumble, "Just shut the door. We don't need anything else."

"Oh, sorry," was all she could manage. *What is wrong with me? Why can't I do anything right?*

She filled a second plate and cautiously made her way into the living room where her stepdaughter and her friends were chatting away before they began their movie. Not quite as bold this time, she stepped into the room as her head began to pound.

Please, please, don't screw this one up too.

The talking stopped. All eyes shifted to her.

Nancy made eye contact with her stepdaughter, who smiled and nodded.

Did she just smile? Do not freak out! Just set them down and leave!

When she put the plate on the end table by her stepdaughter, she took a deep breath and said, "Oh, Nancy, these smell wonderful."

It wasn't a "thank you." It wasn't a "get out of here" either. Maybe things were not as horrible as she thought.

A few weeks later, Nancy carried her stepdaughter's laundry basket filled with clean clothes down the hallway. When she saw that her bedroom door was open, she lightly knocked. Her stepdaughter looked up from the book she was reading and waved Nancy into her room.

Setting the basket on the floor by her bed, Nancy asked, "Is that a new book?"

"Yeah, it's the first nonfiction book I've ever read."

"What's it about? Do you like it so far?"

Their conversation continued, and Nancy made plans with her stepdaughter to have a little book club, just the two of them. It was fascinating to see how just by asking a simple question, they ended up with a plan to learn about themselves with the help of a new book. Nancy began to understand that she didn't have to create grand gestures to be a part of her stepchildren's lives. She just had to show up as herself.

Impact

Your past is impacting your present, whether you know it or not. Sometimes people don't think about how their daily lives growing up impact them as adults. Your culture affects who you become and how you see the world, so when you consider your culture, go deeper than your ethnicity or race.

Think about your family dynamics, your daily routines, and the overall environment of your upbringing. It usually isn't until you move out of your childhood home when you begin to notice that the things you thought were normal may not necessarily be as common to everyone else, and vice versa.

For Victoria, growing up as an only child in a single-parent household affected the way she viewed money. There was never enough for the things they needed, and that drove her to seek a job that could give her financial stability.

Growing up without her father, Victoria didn't have a healthy male role model, which led her to seek more male friends. Her past created stress and anxiety in her life, which she began to understand and work through, once she learned how her past impacted her life as an adult.

Nancy's relationship with her mother was almost the opposite of Victoria's experience. Having her mom as her best friend led Nancy to believe she should work as hard as she possibly could to earn the love and appreciation of her stepchildren. It was difficult for her to understand why her stepchildren did not seem to like her even though she was doing everything for them.

She assumed that since her husband had full custody of his children, they would love her automatically because she was their stepmom. She discovered that the impact of her beautiful relationship with her mother created the belief that when she became a mom, things would be as easy and natural as they were for her.

With a stepfather of her own, who was mostly in the background, Nancy began her marriage accepting the fact that her soon-to-be-retired husband would come and go as he pleased, and she would be the one to take care of everything, including his kids. As time went on, she began to resent him for his lack of involvement, but she wasn't sure how to address her feelings with him.

My family moved around a lot when I was younger, between Mexico and the United States. My parents separated when I was just a year and a half. My last memory of my dad was going out for pizza when I was four years old. After that, he was gone. He never reached out, even though I tried to look for him over the years. It wasn't until my thirty-fourth birthday that he finally called me. After three decades of silence, after all those life events without him, the phone call came out of nowhere.

Growing up without my dad left a deep impact on me, even in ways I didn't fully realize at the time. There was sadness, of course, but also a lingering feeling of rejection. It showed up in unexpected places, like walking into a room and instantly feeling like I didn't belong, or keeping people at arm's length so I wouldn't be hurt first. I started to believe that men couldn't be trusted and there was no reason to respect them. Before anyone could reject me, I would reject them. It took me a long time to understand that these patterns were rooted in that early wound. It's a wound I am still learning to heal with compassion and honesty. All while continuing to build a relationship with my dad and his family due to his continued efforts to have me in his life now.

Observe

Now that you have seen how our past can impact our present, let's look within. When you can become an observer, it helps you gain perspective as you look at your life from a bird's-eye view. We have opportunities to learn from everything that happens, whether good or bad. It can help you appreciate the good things and look for the lessons and opportunities for growth from the bad things. That helps you see a full life. Understanding that you can use the power within you to live the life you want—no matter what happened in the past—is an empowering lesson we all deserve to learn.

Let's also observe your culture and where you come from so you can improve your self-awareness and understand the influence of your past. Think about how you grew up and what that environment was like.

- Were your parents at home when you got back from school?
- How did they interact with each other and with you?
- Did you have family dinners around the dining room table or other routines or family time?
- What were the traditions you shared with your family?
- How involved were you in your community?
- How would you describe your friend group growing up?

In the circle on the next page, imagine it represents your entire life, including all the things that have happened to you—the good and the bad. Would you say your life is a fifty-fifty blend of amazing things and painful things? Is it more like a sixty-forty split? Give yourself some time to consider the ratio and draw a line to show the two different sides, then label them "good" and "bad."

Now we will observe as we put it on paper. Use words, symbols, or drawings. On the "bad" side, show all the things you are trying to heal, those things you wish didn't happen to you, and the things you don't think you deserved. Then turn your focus to the good side. Add all those memories that bring a smile to your face—the moments you cherish and want more of, the times you felt really happy, when you accomplished something you were proud of, and the times when your efforts were celebrated.

Once your circle is complete, look at each moment and ask yourself, "How does my past impact me today?"

With this awareness, you can clearly see what you still need to work on and what gets to be celebrated more. For example, Nancy gets to celebrate that she is a great mom, she gets to feel grateful for building a healthy relationship with her stepdaughter, and she gets to feel proud for the incredible relationships she has with her students. When you

When you can find ways to focus on the good things, you can see that it's not just thorns in this valley of roses.

can find ways to focus on the good things, you can see that it's not just thorns in this valley of roses.

And if it is hard to think of the good things in your life right now, here are some questions you can ask yourself:

- Describe the last time you experienced a moment of pure joy.
- What makes you feel at peace?
- Who or what makes you feel loved, even in this moment?
- What is one thing that is working in your life right now?
- If my pain could speak with kindness, what would it want me to remember about who I am?

Congratulations, I am so proud of you! You took the time to review your past. I know that it isn't an easy thing to do, but you did it!

Release

It's normal to feel uncomfortable as you bring your past to the surface. You may start to feel physical reactions as you revisit specific memories or events. Some common reactions could be feeling a knot in your throat, stomach discomfort, your chest feeling tight, your shoulders and back feeling hot or tense, or getting a headache. These physical sensations are the result of the unaddressed emotions that were stored in your body over time. Below are some helpful tools to help you manage the physical symptoms of your emotions.

If your past brings up feelings that are too extreme for you to manage on your own, please seek out a professional counselor, therapist, or psychologist to help you work through them. Having someone to talk to who can listen to you and give you a different perspective is a great way to feel safe and supported as you work through your past together. If you need immediate support because you are having thoughts of self-harm, pick up your phone and dial 988 in the US.

As you notice different feelings overflowing while you work through your past in this section, it's important to express them in a healthy way. I've included some helpful emotional regulation techniques below. Try each one, and notice how they make you feel. Once you identify your favorites, come back to them whenever you need to.

Diaphragmatic Breathing

This breathwork technique is also known as belly breathing. It helps you slow down and focus on taking deep breaths instead of breathing shallow into your chest. Slowly inhale through your nose, letting your abdomen expand as much as possible. Then exhale through your nose or mouth—whatever makes you feel more comfortable—allowing your abdomen to fully contract as it becomes flat. This technique can activate your body's relaxation response, giving you a sense of peace while reducing your stress levels.

Box Breathing

You may have heard of this technique that Navy SEALs have used in their training. Also called square breathing, you inhale, hold your breath, exhale, then hold your breath again before repeating the cycle. As you go through the steps, choose an equal count of time. For example, you may inhale for four seconds, hold for four, exhale for four, then hold again. Practicing box breathing can help slow down your breathing, increase your mindfulness and ability to be present, and reduce stress and anxiety.

Alternate Nostril Breathing

This is a breathing technique that can help balance your nervous system and calm your mind. For this one, you'll shift from breathing through your left and right nostrils, using your fingers to block one side at a time. Start by using your right thumb to close your right nostril as you inhale through your left nostril, then use your right index finger to close your left nostril as you exhale through your right nostril. Then reverse the pattern, inhaling through your right nostril and exhaling through your left. This technique can also help you feel grounded, relaxed, and clearheaded.

Punching a Pillow

Instead of causing harm to yourself or someone else, punching a pillow is a safe way to express anger, frustration, or stress. You can set your pillow on your bed or lap, and as you punch it, express the stored emotions that have been stuck inside you. It also helps with releasing physical tension in your body.

Moving Your Body

Sometimes the best way to get out of your head is to move your body after setting an intention to let go of the strong feelings you are feeling and releasing any discomfort you want to work through. Movement can come in the form of going for a walk or a run, dancing, stretching, or moving in a favorite class that interests you.

Connecting with Others

Creating relationships with others can be a great way to give and receive support. Engaging in meaningful experiences and having conversations with others can help everyone involved process emotions, gain new perspectives, and feel less isolated. You can connect with people you know by calling a friend or getting together in person. You can also connect with people you don't know yet by joining a local group or a new community online. This is especially beneficial if you tend to isolate yourself when you are struggling. Give yourself the opportunity to be helped.

Experiencing Nature

By allowing yourself to experience nature, you can feel more grounded and connected to the world around you. It can also help you practice being more present as you notice the wildlife around you. Nature walks can provide an incredible feeling of peace. The next time you find yourself outside, take a moment to notice the flowers or birds around you, and just breathe.

Grounding

Also called earthing, it is a great way to find peace when you feel overwhelmed. Go outside and walk barefoot on grass, sit under a tree, or touch any plant on the ground. When you connect your body directly to the earth, your nervous system relaxes, and it becomes easier to stay present.

Releasing

Take your emotions and externalize them instead of keeping them stored inside you. You can do this by talking to someone and releasing what is in your heart and mind as you speak. You can also use a journal to put your feelings on the paper. Releasing our emotions in a healthy way can set us free.

As you continue to release, I want you to keep a visual in mind:

Imagine for a moment that you carry a cup inside you. It's a sacred vessel that holds all your emotions, experiences, memories, and unspoken pain. Over the years, this cup had quietly collected rain from the dark clouds of the past: old wounds, unprocessed grief, rejection, shame, and anger. Some of it settled at the bottom. Some of it rose to the top. Now it's full to overflowing, not because you're weak, but because you've carried so much for so long without releasing it.

Instead of shutting down or saying, "I can't take any more," you can honor yourself enough to stop pushing the hard stuff down and start letting it rise to come out of the cup. When the darker rain begins to surface, don't turn away from it. Notice it. Breathe through it. Release it, layer by layer. As you do, you make space for something new to flow in: lightness, clarity, truth, and peace. The cup within you was never meant to stay full of what weighs you down. It was meant to be emptied, rinsed, and refilled with what heals you.

Now that you have given yourself time to think about where you come from, observe your life without judgment, and release what no longer serves you. It's time to look at how you can use your past to move you forward in chapter 4.

Chapter Four

The Power of Perspective

Gaby expertly flicked her wrists to open the next tablecloth and watched it float perfectly onto the table in her backyard. She had to cover five more tables and get the centerpieces on them before their guests began to arrive in an hour. The kids had already unfolded the chairs, placed them around the tables, and escaped to their rooms. The menu had been set a week ago, and all the timers were doing their jobs as the fellowship meal cooked in her kitchen.

Once the tables were set, she took some pictures and posted them on her social media account with the caption, "Ready for some fun with the church fam?"

Perfect. I just need to remember to post the recipes and pictures of the food once it's ready.

Her husband was at another neighbor's house helping them with a leak under their kitchen sink.

He'll be home in time to shower before anyone gets here. If he's a little late, everyone will understand. After all, we're the family that all our neighbors can count on to lend a helping hand.

For a moment, she reflected on her own childhood. Her mom was an incredible homemaker and cook who loved sharing sweet treats with her neighbors. Her dad worked hard as a carpenter, and when a neighbor needed a handyman, they knew they could count on him. Always smiling, never complaining, always kind and helpful—that's how people viewed Gaby and her family.

Gaby followed along with her family's example—get married, have a baby, then another, and then another. As a forty-two-year-old with a husband and three children of her own, Gaby took her parents' practice of loving her neighbors seriously. She put a lot of time and effort into her social media posts, showing the world her beautiful family and sharing her dessert recipes that got her a lot of followers and comments. From her social media posts to the church gatherings at their home, Gaby was a good wife and mother with a good family.

So if I have everything I've always wanted, why do I feel so empty?

She could hear the first timer going off inside, so she adjusted the final centerpiece and scurried into the kitchen, leaving that thought behind.

As always, the get-together was a huge success. Everyone loved the latest menu items, and a few of the other women asked for the recipes.

Good thing I printed copies yesterday.

After their guests said their goodbyes and went home, her family scattered. Her kids mumbled to one another as they went into their bedrooms and shut their doors. Her husband slumped away into his office, mentioning some work thing she didn't know about that needed his attention before the next day. Gaby was exhausted from all the preparations and then socializing with a smile on her face for hours.

As she worked on tidying up the house, she wondered, *Did my mom feel the same back when she was the designated all-time hostess for their church gatherings?* She immediately felt guilty for letting that thought cross her mind. *After all, loving my neighbors should be my number one priority. If that was the case, why do I feel like I'm living a lie, always pretending to be happy when I feel so miserable inside?* She deliberately shook her head. *I'm just tired. It's been a long day.*

As those thoughts popped up, she'd say a prayer and do the best she could to get ready for her next obligation and hide the sadness her face worked so hard to conceal. She went through a mental list of things she should be grateful for, then shamed herself for being anything but happy with the life she had.

But it didn't make her feel any better. It actually made her feel worse and even more alone and empty in a home filled with people she was supposed to take care of.

That Monday, Gaby met with her mom for a scheduled lunch date. After talking about their weekends, instead of their typical conversation about which desserts they would prepare for the next weekend gathering, her mom handed her an envelope.

"Gaby, I see myself in you, and I wanted to give you some time to take a break and do something for yourself."

"I don't understand."

"I wasn't the best role model for you. I felt so alone, I pretended like I was happy when I wasn't, and I didn't realize what I was doing until I started working on myself. This women's retreat changed my life, and I just know it can help you if you go into it with an open mind."

Her mom had already talked to Gaby's husband, and they made all the arrangements together. She didn't have to worry about the kids getting to school or practice. Another family volunteered to host the next weekend gathering. All she had to do was pack and go to the airport for a weeklong retreat. So with a true feeling of gratitude in her heart, Gaby went home and packed for her flight out that evening.

Although she dealt with some guilt on the plane for leaving her family for a whole week, Gaby had an incredible time at the retreat. She began to realize that she didn't have to relive her mother's life; it was time to break the pattern.

After working on the different exercises and learning how to practice self-love, Gaby flew home with the understanding that she could choose a different future for herself and her family. Her biggest takeaway was that she had to take care of herself first to be able to be there for her kids and husband instead of forgetting about herself and feeling sad, lonely, resentful, and guilty.

She came home with a new understanding about how she was showing up in her relationships, with her husband and each of her children. She had a new plan to observe and become more aware of the way she interacted with them. She promised herself that she'd keep learning and growing so she could prioritize herself and strengthen her family, beginning with her husband and their strained relationship. She created the awareness that she needed to pour onto herself first.

Evolving

I believe that your past does not have to predict your future. You can choose to perceive it as a learning experience instead of something detrimental that continuously affects your life. You can let your past continue to hurt you and make you believe that you are a victim, you deserve to suffer, or you aren't good enough to have a good

> *You can evolve into feeling certain that you deserve love, peace, and joy.*

life. Or you can decide that you are worthy of a better life, because you are. Healing requires evolving. You can evolve into feeling certain that you deserve love, peace, and joy.

In *Change Your Life, Change Your Paradigm*, Bob Proctor talks about changing our deep rooted beliefs. He explains that unless we become aware of them and change our repeated habits, we'll keep getting the same results. Consider the possibility that you are not healing because of the beliefs you've been carrying. What if you can evolve into choosing happiness, peace, and healing?

Dr. Wayne Dyer, another one of my favorite authors, talked about changing our perspective to have a better life. His famous quote "When you change the way you look at things, the things you look at change" is a reminder of how powerful the tool of changing our perspective is. When we begin to see our pain with compassion instead of shame, our patterns with curiosity instead of judgment, and our past with love, everything starts to flow. Perspective becomes the doorway to peace.

You can practice the ability to look deep within yourself and acknowledge that you are meant for a better life. That longing you feel inside is there for a reason. It's telling you that you are worthy of more and that you have the ability to achieve it. But growth isn't always easy, and healing doesn't happen overnight. There will be days when self-doubt creeps in, when old patterns try to pull you back, and when you feel like you can't do it on your own. Remember that you don't have to.

Reaching out for support isn't a sign of weakness. It's part of the process and a powerful act of self-awareness and self-compassion. Whether it's a friend, mentor, therapist, or a community who understands you, allow yourself to be supported. Keep reminding yourself that you aren't alone, your journey is valid, and you can keep moving forward.

Assertiveness

Assertiveness is communicating in a way that is calm and respectful while still asking for what you need. It's not about being aggressive or demanding, and it's not about staying quiet to avoid conflict. It's about taking a step back, recognizing how you feel, and then expressing it in a way that makes it more likely for others to listen. Sometimes we doubt our ability to be assertive because our self-esteem is so low that we forget we have a voice. We may also struggle with feeling unworthy to speak our mind.

There is a difference between your worth and your self-esteem. To me, your worth is always the same. At times, you may forget and lose sight of who you truly are at your core. Think about taking a dollar bill and crumbling it into a ball, then flattening it out again. It is still a dollar bill, with a few creases and folds, but its value doesn't change. On the other hand, your self-esteem could lower based on how you think about what you deserve in life, but it can also increase depending on the way you choose to see yourself and the relationship you have with yourself.

When you were a child, your worth and self-esteem worked together in perfect harmony. You didn't have room for thinking that you were anything less than incredible. You naturally knew how to live in the present, how to speak up for what you wanted, and how to embrace those moments of pure joy. As you got older, you started to listen to others more than your inner self. Comparison set in, and your self-esteem began to lessen over time. But it doesn't have to be that way.

When we have spent years being passive, thinking about being assertive can feel scary and overwhelming. Sometimes in trying to stand up for ourselves, we overcompensate and can come off more forceful than we anticipated. Assertiveness takes practice, and it is about finding the right balance for you. It is about learning to express your needs clearly, and with time, it will become a natural way to honor yourself and your needs.

Gaby began to notice that after everyone left her gatherings, she was the only one cleaning up. She'd stand in her kitchen, exhausted from hosting, looking at the mess with resentment building inside her. Then she'd automatically feel guilty for feeling that way because she knew that serving others was something she was supposed to do.

After taking a step back, she began to understand what was really happening. She wasn't upset with her friends. She was upset with herself for never asking for help. She assumed that people should just know they should help, but the truth was, they couldn't read her mind. Instead of staying in a cycle of frustration and guilt, she decided to communicate differently and practice being assertive.

The next time she hosted a get-together, she sent out a message earlier that morning, letting them know that she felt overwhelmed after everyone left the last time and asking for a few volunteers to stay behind for about fifteen minutes to help with the clean-up. Another time, she explained that she was feeling drained by hosting every time and asked if they could create a hosting rotation. After sending those two messages, Gaby was amazed at how many people wanted to lend a hand with cleaning and hosting.

Being assertive didn't mean demanding that people help. It didn't mean assuming they should already know what she needed. It meant being honest with herself, recognizing that she needed support, and expressing herself clearly. Gaby was able to shift her focus from hoping others would volunteer without her asking to feeling proud of herself for speaking up.

Gaby began to understand that tuning into herself, recognizing what she needed, and asking for it in a way that respected herself and those around her was a new tool she could use when she noticed herself feeling overwhelmed or frustrated.

If you are struggling with being assertive, try this: Think about your childhood photos. If you have access to them, take a moment to find one that was taken on a day when you felt happy. If not, take a moment to see yourself as a child in your mind's eye. When you talk to yourself about the life you want from now on, think about what you would say to that younger version of yourself. Would you tell her that she doesn't deserve to ask for what she needs? Of course you wouldn't. You know the little girl in the picture deserves to speak up and have an incredible life.

I invite you to keep a picture of your younger self with you. It could be the wallpaper on your phone or a framed picture that you keep in your home so that you can consistently look at it whenever you find yourself doubting that your needs are valid. Remember, she is you, and your voice matters. Every time you speak with clarity, you reclaim a part of yourself. You got this!

Empowerment

> *When we trust, it becomes easier to see things from a place of growth instead of fear.*

Empowerment begins the moment you choose to see your life through a new lens. It's recognizing that we have the power to change how we see things. More than that, empowerment is also about trust—trusting ourselves, trusting the process, trusting God or the universe, and trusting your healing path. When we trust, it becomes easier to see things from a place of growth instead of fear.

When I recently went to Mexico to visit my mom, I needed to get some fillings in my teeth. The first one was done by an experienced dentist, and everything went well with no major issues. A few days later, I went back for a second filling, but the first dentist I worked with had to go out of town. He reassured me that a newly graduated dentist could do it and that she was ready and capable. I decided I'd be fine with the newer dentist.

But after the filling was complete, something didn't feel right. I went back the next day and explained my concerns, and she ended up redoing the filling.

At first, my mind began to spiral, *What if she doesn't know what she's doing? What if this falls out? Will I need a crown?*

I got caught up in catastrophizing.

I stopped, took a deep breath, and realized I was only hurting myself by thinking that way. I had a choice to make. I could keep holding on to the fear, or I could trust and choose empowerment.

I thought, *Maybe this experience is helping her learn and improve. Maybe she's realizing that she needs to take her time and be more careful the first time. Since she redid it, it can actually be better for me in the long run. I trust my path. I was assertive and communicated my worries to her.*

The shift in my perspective changed everything. I suddenly didn't feel frustrated anymore. I wasn't as anxious about everything that could go wrong. Instead, I felt at ease. When I stopped to pay attention, I realized that my tooth didn't feel uncomfortable anymore.

By trusting that it was going to work out, it became easier to shift my mindset. Empowerment isn't about making everything go exactly the way we want it to. It's about knowing that no matter what happens, we have the power to shape the meaning of it in a way that best serves us.

Let's Reflect

You now have seen the power of perspective—let's take a moment to apply it. Think of an event or situation that was frustrating or triggering. Write it down, and consider your initial thought. Then let's change it to a new perspective. Think of an empowering way you can see it. When you become more aware of your patterns, the shift to a new perspective becomes easier.

Past Event	Initial Thought	New Perspective
Carla: My filling wasn't right.	What a mess! Am I going to lose my tooth?	By going back and explaining that it doesn't feel right, I can help her learn and grow. I trust that this is a learning experience for both of us.
Gaby: These women never helped; they were so rude.	I shouldn't judge them. I just need to do it all.	I trust myself to ask for what I need. I am deserving of help and support.

You:		

With a perspective that works for you, anything is possible.

I am proud of you for taking the time to dive deeper into your past and choosing to ask yourself, "How does my past affect me today?" and "How can I grow from it?" You realized that even though looking at our past is uncomfortable, it is a necessary step in our healing journey.

As we move from the lessons of the past into our present, remember that the power is within you to create an incredible life.

For a Moment

For a moment, I wake up in fear.
I am consumed with all the pain and sorrow.
I feel empty and wonder if relief is near.

For a moment, I remember all the suffering that brought me here,
To this moment that is so hard to believe.
Do I have enough power within? Why am I here?

For a moment, I wish I was gone, or lost, or left alone.
I cry and wonder when all will be forgotten.
I want it all gone—the pain, the suffering,
oh, what have I become?

For a moment, I become aware
that being in my head is exhausting.
Depression? Anxiety? Is this my reality?
The thoughts are overwhelming and I'm drowning.

For a moment, I remember who I am.
I'm awake and I can see what I am meant to be.
I find the strength, and I believe in me.

For a moment, I know that I must keep going.
I remember that I am strong, independent, and free.
I must love and accept myself, because in the end, this is part of
my soul's growing.

For a moment, I know that this is me,
With the ups and downs, with the pride and guilt,
with the love and hate
This is me, and for a moment, peace is in me.

—Carla Calderas

As I continued my healing journey, I was more aware of my feelings and the impact of my past. I was also noticing that I was starting to have great days and feelings of peace. I wrote this poem as a reminder that feelings are temporary, and as humans, we will experience all of them. While I was healing and doing the emotional work, sadness, frustration, and anger were still coming out of me, and I needed to remember that these feelings were just for a moment.

We are going to have moments of doubt. In those moments, it is important to remind ourselves about how far we have come. As we heal, we will also experience moments of happiness and peace.

PART TWO

THE
PRESENT

Chapter Five

Your Power Is in the Present

Now that you've taken the opportunity to explore your past and learn more about Victoria, Nancy, and Gaby, it's time to take action in the present. We are going to take a closer look at how you can put in the intentional work to create positive shifts in your life.

Lasting change occurs when you become aware of your thoughts, feelings, and behaviors. Once you begin creating some awareness about your patterns of behavior, you can decide what you want for your life by evaluating what is and isn't working for you. From that space, you can begin to focus and invest your energy on aligning your thoughts, feelings, and behaviors to match how you want your life to be. Remember, healing is a journey rather than a destination, and staying consistent with new exercises and tools can help keep you on the right path.

Your thoughts, feelings, and behaviors are connected. Maybe you think you look off today. Your jeans feel tight, you feel bloated, but you still have to go to the store.

You think, *I look awful. I should have stayed home. What if I see someone I know? How embarrassing!*

Once you get to the store, you look down and avoid eye contact. You assume that others are judging how you look. You may even wonder if they think they're better than you. Those thoughts then lead to feelings of worthlessness, rejection, sadness, and even depression. With those feelings come behaviors that match them—rushing through the store to avoid being seen or popping your earbuds in and looking at your phone instead of trying to connect with others.

As you can see, the way you think about the world around you will influence your reality in both positive and negative ways. On your journey of healing, the first step is to identify the thought you are having and remind yourself that you can change it. If you can change the thought, it helps you feel hopeful, builds your self-esteem, and change the way you live your life. Consider the connection between the thoughts, feelings, and behaviors in the following scenario.

The alarm clock blares, and your body jolts you awake again. You keep your eyes closed as you reach for the phone on the nightstand. Once you decide you can't hit the Snooze button one more time, you find yourself shuffling into the bathroom.

"Ugh. I just woke up, and I'm already exhausted."

There's no way you're going to look in the mirror as you brush your teeth.

Thoughts swirl around in your head as you turn on the shower: *I don't want to go to work today. I can't stay home. I'm too poor to quit.*

In the shower, your thoughts shift to your body:

Oh, look at these folds in my stomach. I'm getting so fat. My skin is so dull.

Your shoulders slump as you glance into your closet.

"Nothing fits right anymore. What am I going to wear?"

You finally make a choice, throw it on, and run out the door. There's no time for breakfast because you took so long trying to look halfway decent.

Traffic is awful, as usual, and you find yourself yelling at all the horrible drivers around you on the way to work.

Walking up to the building, you're mumbling what you consider a little pep talk to yourself about all the things that are wrong with your coworkers. You wonder what you can do to avoid them. You don't have to worry about your coworkers today though. They're used to avoiding you because you know they don't like you. But you don't care, and you try to hide this with an inauthentic smile as you make your way into your office. Closing your office door shut—hoping nobody knocks—indicates the start of your workday.

When it comes to your thoughts, feelings, and behaviors, it is important to understand that you always have a choice. It sounds almost too good to be true, but you can train yourself to choose to have a good day based on what you decide to focus on. Let's look at that same morning as though you are choosing to have a "glass-half-full" kind of day.

The alarm on your phone plays soft music and birdsongs. You take a second to stretch your body from your fingertips to your toes, turn off the alarm, and head for the bathroom. You greet yourself in the mirror with a sleepy smile.

"I'm feeling a little tired this morning. I need to remember to go to bed a little earlier tonight. I am so proud of myself for taking the time to choose my outfit last night and meal prepping on Sunday. It makes weekday mornings run smoothly without the rush."

You turn on the shower and start thinking, *I am grateful for the job I have. I know it affords me the lifestyle I have. Today I choose to make it a peaceful day.*

In the shower, your thoughts shift to your body:

I choose to love my body. This is where I am right now, and it's a good starting point. If I want to change how I look, I know some things I can do. I am worthy of a healthy body.

You slip into the dress that you chose the night before and give yourself a little twirl.

"I love this dress! Today I am choosing joy."

You have some extra time after doing your hair and makeup, so you start listening to the next episode of your favorite podcast as you eat breakfast at your kitchen table.

Traffic is awful, as usual, but you find yourself smiling as you continue listening to the podcast in your car. Maybe you are becoming the change you wish to see.

Walking into the building, you smile, knowing that your colleagues are on their own healing journeys. You realize that judgments seem to be disappearing as you continue to work on yourself. Today you choose to focus on what you can control and on being a light in the world. You chat with your team about the next steps in the project you're working on and leave your office door open in case they have any questions, knowing that you are in charge of your day.

> *A big part of being able to have the fulfilling life you deserve is how you choose to see yourself and the world around you.*

Getting to the point where you are living with a better outlook is going to take time, and that is part of the journey. A big part of being able to have the fulfilling life you deserve is how you choose to see yourself and the world around you. When you can take control of your thoughts throughout the day, your entire world can change for the better. Let's continue.

Focus

Think about all the things that are worrying you right now. Are these things that you can adjust or are responsible for? Or are these out of your control because they involve other people or outside circumstances? Many times when we focus on the things that are out of our control, we feel powerless and overwhelmed. It is important to remember that if we focus on the things we can control, we're going to get our power back. Working through the Circles of Control activity can help us put our worries into perspective.

Think of a target with three circles. The biggest circle contains the things we would like to control but can't. Weather, traffic, and what other people think of us all fit into the biggest circle.

The medium circle has the things that you can influence. This includes the treatment we accept from our family, our part in relationships, and the healing environment we create with others. We can do our part as we share our thoughts and make suggestions, but it is up to them whether they choose to act on your influence or not.

The smallest circle is for the things you have one-hundred-percent control over. Notice that this is your target and where you want your focus. It represents the power within you. It's filled with your thoughts, reactions, responses to people and situations that happen to you.

Let's begin by looking at how Gaby and I would complete this activity if we sat down to work on it together.

On her biggest circle, she could list things like "people at church gossiping about me," "the weather," and "traffic." These are all things that Gaby can only respond to instead of control. If she knows the traffic on her way to a certain place always takes longer than planned, she can decide to leave her house earlier. For the weather, she could check an app ahead of time to know what to wear or whether she needs to take an umbrella to her son's game. As for people talking about her, I would point out that she doesn't have any control over what they say, but she does have control over what she says to and about them. She also gets to decide whether she wants to spend her time with them outside of church or not, without beating herself up over having less get-togethers. She could then use that time to be more present with her own family.

In her medium circle, Gaby could write: "frequency of sex between me and my husband" and "my son playing baseball instead of basketball." She could talk to her husband and her son about those items and may be able to influence their decisions with her opinions, but I would remind her that asking and demanding are two very different things. You can influence someone's choices, but you can't make them do what you want just because you shared your thoughts with them. We would discuss that a request from her doesn't mean a "yes" from the other person, and getting a "no" isn't a failure on her part. She gets to celebrate expressing her concerns and starting a healthy conversation.

In her smallest circle, Gaby could add, "the way I talk to my husband," "how I communicate with my kids," and "my physical appearance." I would then explore how she has the power to choose words that work for her and not against her, reinforcing that she can allow herself to be more aware of the words she chooses during those conversations. She could tell me what she would like to say, and we would work together to improve what she has said in the past. Then we could have a conversation about her physical appearance, what she likes and dislikes about it. All this coming from a place of gratitude of where she is, hope, and actionable steps for where she wants to be.

Now let's practice. Use the graphic below to help you focus on what you can control, influence what you can, and let go of what is out of your control.

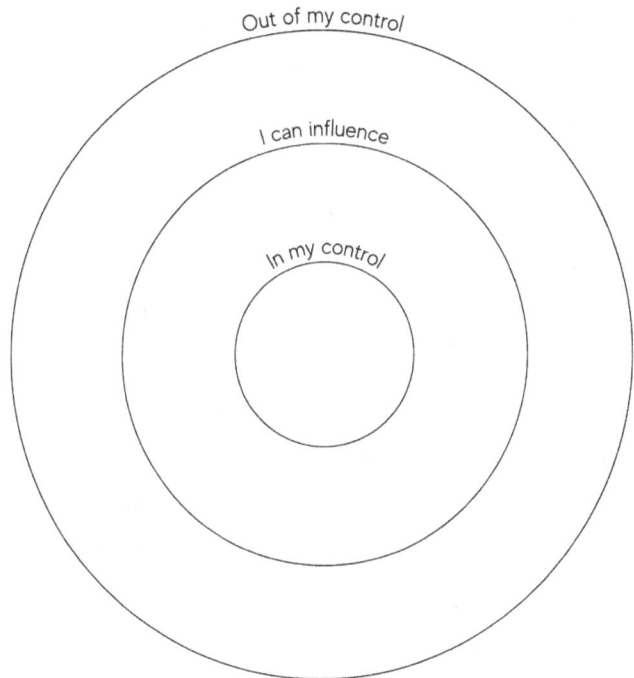

Celebrate

As you continue your healing journey, you may notice that all your efforts lie in improving. With that mindset, it is difficult to take the time to celebrate your growth. As a chronic overachiever, I know that it can be easy for us to try and live in the future by constantly looking for the next goal we want to achieve.

I want to encourage you to celebrate your progress as you notice it. As you move through your days, allow yourself to look at what you handle well. Then take some time to celebrate that! It can be anything from giving yourself a well-deserved break by going to your favorite park to simply smiling at your reflection and thinking to yourself, "Wow. Great job!" Other examples include journaling and writing yourself a love letter, creating a list of all these wins to refer back to, and making healthy and healing choices for your mind and body.

During my healing journey, I became aware that I was using food to comfort me. I remember the very first time it happened as a little girl. I was upset, and I was given a big glass of chocolate milk and some pancakes in the afternoon. I realized that in that moment, that event taught me to reach for food anytime I was uncomfortable. Now that I understand this pattern in my behavior, I get to choose something different to relieve my stress and create lasting change. I may go for a walk in nature, call my mom and talk to her, or anything else that fills me up.

> *Each time I make a better choice, I get to celebrate it!*

Each time I make a better choice, I get to celebrate it! I tell you this story to give you insight and create awareness about your behaviors. Ask yourself, "Am I celebrating with a healthy behavior that is aligned with the best version of myself?"

If you are not, you have a choice! Choose a celebration that is healing.

Celebrate that you are making different choices now and are becoming aware of your patterns. You got this!

Now

Before we move forward, I want to pause and bring our focus to this moment, right here, right now. That's what this section is all about: learning to stay present. It might seem simple, but if you're anything like me, you've probably noticed how often your mind wants to pull you elsewhere. Maybe it drifts back into the past, replaying pain, guilt or what could have been. Or maybe it skips ahead into the future, trying to plan every detail or brace for what might go wrong. Either way, the one place we rarely settle into is the now. But this section is your invitation to change that.

The power of the present is more than just a title. It's a reminder that this moment, the one you're in right now, is where all your strength lives. Your healing is not hiding in the past. Your breakthroughs won't wait for some far-off tomorrow. It all begins in the now. And the more we can bring ourselves back to this space, the more peace and clarity we'll start to find. Your healing is taking place now.

That doesn't mean it's going to be easy. Learning to stay present takes practice. It's a habit, one we lost touch with as we grew up. We've learned to escape the present by living in the past or the future. But now we're doing something different. We're retraining the mind. And like any other muscle, it takes time and repetition. So when you catch yourself drifting, whether you're lost in the past or spiraling into the what-ifs of the future, that's your cue to gently redirect yourself back into the moment you're in.

One of the best ways to do this is by using your senses. Ask yourself, "What can I see right now? Can I hear the wind or the sounds around me? What do I taste when I drink or eat this? How does the air feel on my skin?"

Breathe, and let those small, simple details anchor you. Maybe it's a hot cup of tea or the feeling of sunlight on your face. These moments matter. They bring you back home to your body, your breath, and your presence.

It's also important to understand how our minds naturally resist the present when we're struggling. Depression often pulls into the past, reminding us of what's gone wrong, what hurt us, or what we regret. Anxiety, on the other hand, launches us into the future, worrying about what might happen, what might go wrong, or whether we'll be okay.

In neither of those places does your healing live. Therapy can help us process the stories from the past and release the fears about the future, but the real transformation begins when we root ourselves in today.

So as you move into the present, I invite you to be kind to yourself. Don't expect perfection. Just notice. Gently bring your awareness back to the present moment, again and again. Because this moment is your power. This moment is your chance to start fresh. This moment is enough.

Let's dive deeper into understanding our thoughts and how to begin to turn unhealthy thoughts into healthy ones in the next chapter.

Chapter Six

Managing Your Thoughts

Walking up to her front door after a long day at work, Victoria gratefully took a deep breath as she looked for the keys inside her purse. She felt good knowing that she could choose to enter her home with peace. As she stepped over the threshold, her purse bumped the doorframe and swung back at just the right angle to knock the water bottle out of her hand.

She immediately thought, *Ugh, I'm so stupid*, while leaning down to pick it up. She paused to wonder why she said things like that to herself—and how it became a normal part of her everyday life.

Many women struggle with negative self-talk and are left wondering why they do this to themselves. Think about what it looks like when a child knows they are the most incredible person on the planet. Maybe you've seen it in a kid you love or in a moment from your own past, or maybe it's something you've always longed for.

It's not arrogance—it's pure, unfiltered self-love. There's a natural ease in the way children explore the world when they feel safe, loved, and seen. Every new experience sparks wide-eyed wonder. Their belly laughs burst out with joy, lighting up the room and pulling others into the moment, even if they didn't know why you were laughing. That kind of energy is contagious. So . . . what happened?

Your self-talk became what you heard externally. It is heavily influenced by the people you grew up around and the way they spoke to you and each other. As a child, you were so impressionable, and what happened in your home became your baseline for what you consider to be normal.

If your parents said things like, "You're so stupid. You're never going to amount to anything." It's understandable that it got ingrained in you and became the way you speak to yourself. However, now we know where it is coming from, and we can change it. We don't have to repeat the pattern of believing what others, including friends or family, have told us. You have the power to manage your thoughts.

> *It is time to release what no longer serves you so that you can become the person you truly are.*

As you develop the awareness about your thoughts, healing will continue to occur. You don't have to let what you experienced shape you.

It is time to release what no longer serves you so that you can become the person you truly are. You can make a shift by choosing a better way to talk to yourself, starting today.

First, let's look at some common ways that our thoughts can lead us into unhealthy territory.

Scenarios

When you are faced with uncertainty, your brain loves to fill in the blanks and formulate answers. This is where scenarios come into play. Many times, when you lived through a difficult past that included a lot of trauma or challenging circumstances, your brain gets used to automatically thinking of the worst-case scenario. It's easy to feel yourself falling into a downward spiral of horrible reasons to explain why something is happening once that first thought begins.

All that stress can be avoided if you know a way to focus your attention away from the worst-case scenario. One way to work on this is to use your imagination to think of the total opposite: the best-case scenario. It's okay if it sounds silly, impossible, or unrealistic. When you think about it, the worst and best outcomes are both possibilities with the same amount of likelihood. What typically happens is something more in the middle of the two.

Consider the following example.

Nancy gets home from school and notices that her husband hasn't arrived home yet. She calls him to check in but he doesn't answer. As she hangs up the phone, her brain automatically goes into the worst-case scenario mode:

He either died in a car crash on his way home or he is cheating on me and spending his time with someone else.

She takes a deep breath. She reminds herself that those scenarios could be a possibility but those thoughts showed up automatically. Instead of giving them more time, she challenges herself to think of a best-case scenario for why he isn't home yet.

She starts to think, *Maybe he just won the lottery and he's buying me a new car right now.* Or, *He's probably planning a big dinner and will tell me all about it once he gets home.*

If you find yourself struggling with an amazing best-case scenario, it may be because the trauma you have struggled through has made them almost impossible to create. If that was the case for Nancy, her best-case scenario could be closer to something like, *Okay, he is stuck in traffic and will be here in ten minutes.* Or, *He decided to pick up a few things at the store on his way home and he'll call me back soon.*

Wherever you are on your healing journey with creating best-case scenarios—whether they're exceptional outcomes or simple explanations—it is okay. Focusing on knowing that there are other possibilities besides the worst-case scenario is a big step forward. Give yourself some time to breathe and wait on the outcome, because you are healing, and there is no need to give yourself unnecessary stress.

Stories

You always look forward to your monthly Sunday brunches with your friend. This brunch is no exception. Over mimosas, you get the chance to catch up on everything happening in each other's lives. Between sharing stories about your kids and her pets, you suddenly remember your daughter has a volleyball game that starts in half an hour. To her surprise, you jump up, toss enough cash on the table to cover the bill and the tip, and mutter your apologies as you rush out of the restaurant.

You settle into the bleachers, grateful that you made it five minutes before the match is set to begin. You text your friend: "Hey, Gina! Brunch was great! Sorry I had to leave quickly. I lost track of time and had to make it to this volleyball match."

You wave your husband and son over to their saved seats and accept the box of concession stand popcorn he offers you.

When you get home after the game, you check your phone. Your friend didn't respond, and the stories in your head begin:

Why is she mad at me? I told her about the match before we ordered. What did I say during brunch that offended her? Oh no. Is she going to cancel letting me meet her new puppy next week? What did I do so I can apologize? This is why I have no friends. Everyone hates me, and I'm going to die all alone.

Two hours later, she responds with, "No worries. Did she win? Can't wait for you to meet Ace next week! He's so cute!"

When you can catch yourself spiraling into those unhealthy thoughts—whether you catch them at the very beginning, at the lowest point, or somewhere in between— take a moment to pause. Ask yourself if the story feels like you are taking on the role of the victim, and if so, remind yourself that you always have a choice and that you are the protagonist of your life. You are creating your own story, and you have the power to create a story that works for you and how you want to feel.

Use your imagination to come up with a more empowering story instead. Using the example above, maybe you start thinking things like, *I trust that I am the best version of myself when I am interacting with my friend Gina. I know I have been a good friend to her, and I attract others who reciprocate the same level of support and communication with me. I trust that she will respond when she has time to be fully present with me. I know that I am capable of having healthy friendships, so if there is something we need to work through, we can do that the next time we talk.*

You can then give her an opportunity to respond, and if you haven't heard back in a few days, empower yourself to be assertive and just ask her, "Hey, I haven't heard from you. Is everything all right?"

Interpretations

How you interpret the world and what happens to you can be based on your past and how others treated you. So let's look at how we can break this pattern. It's important to understand the meaning we create as we experience different events in our lives. Sometimes the way we interpret an event doesn't work for us and is more of a cycle based on our past rather than the actual outcome.

For example, you walk into a party and see Maria from across the room. You remember meeting her last summer. She looks at you and then looks away. Your immediate interpretation is, *Oh, she doesn't like me.*

You can begin by validating that it is okay to have that interpretation of the event, but you can go a step further by asking yourself where it came from. Maybe it's your inner child feeling rejected because it was a common pattern in your past. It can cause you to be hypersensitive to external cues that prove those thoughts to be true, even if the reality of the situation is different from your initial thought.

When faced with an interpretation, you have choices. You can decide that she doesn't like you and avoid her the rest of the night, wondering why and being upset. Another choice is to give yourself and Maria the benefit of the doubt. Maybe she did like you when you first met and she doesn't have a great memory, or perhaps she got distracted by someone else at the party and forgot to approach you.

Your next option is to simply have that conversation from a place of curiosity, explaining a pattern you're noticing. You could begin by saying, "Hey, Maria, I've noticed that when we run into each other, sometimes we don't greet each other. Are you open to improving our relationship?"

Finally, if you notice the pattern continuing, you can decide to not engage with someone who isn't valuing your worth.

Just like stories and scenarios, interpretations take time and practice to shift. Creating lasting change begins with changing your thoughts, starting with your self-talk. Let's dive deeper into this concept.

Shifting

If you're ready to become more aware of your thoughts, begin by observing how you feel throughout your day. Your thoughts are creating your feelings. If you notice that you aren't feeling happy, excited, or passionate about your life and the people in it, you probably aren't having the healthiest thoughts.

Managing your self-talk takes some effort on your part, especially when you aren't used to it. When you can be kinder to yourself in your own mind, it can make your outlook on life brighter. With self-compassion and healthy self-talk, our outlook on life changes to a new perspective where we find opportunities for peace and joy.

Sometimes we don't have the emotional capacity for more empowering self-talk due to trauma, difficult experiences, or living in a difficult environment. It is important to meet yourself where you are. Changing from an unhealthy thought to a healthy one is going to require perseverance.

Developing the awareness of your thoughts takes time. At the beginning, you may be surprised at the amount of unhealthy thoughts that appear in one day. As you continue to practice these skills, you may find that your first unhealthy thought didn't appear until late in the evening. It won't be perfect, but the more you practice shifting your self-talk , the easier it becomes to catch yourself and swap those thoughts over time.

> *With self-compassion and healthy self-talk, our outlook on life changes to a new perspective where we find opportunities for peace and joy.*

Be patient with yourself as you develop this new awareness. Kindness, self-compassion, and gentleness with yourself will get you there.

An easy way to start shifting your self-talk is to ask yourself if you would say those things to a dear friend or to a child.

Imagine you were sitting on a park bench and a little girl walked up to you saying, "Nobody wants to play with me. Nobody likes me."

You probably wouldn't look at her tiny tear-stained face and say, "You feel all alone because you are. Look at you—your clothes are all dirty, you're fat and ugly, and I can't believe you're holding an ice cream cone. You should be exercising instead. As a matter of fact, throw away that cone and start running laps."

More likely, you'd gently wipe her tears, scoop her into your lap, and start building her up. So if you wouldn't talk to a little girl like that, it's time to decide you are worthy of better self-talk too.

It's all about talking to yourself in a kind way. It is important to develop this tool because it can eventually build your self-esteem back up. Remember, your self-esteem is the perception of how much you love yourself and how you align your thoughts and behaviors to reflect this love for yourself. Another way to think about it is matching your worth with your self-esteem, because remember, you are worthy of having all the abundance in the world simply because you are alive. Practicing compassionate self-talk helps you be in a good headspace and can also create improved communication with other people.

When you hear yourself saying those hurtful, unhealthy thoughts, take a moment to remind yourself that they aren't from you. Allow yourself the opportunity to let it go and be kinder to yourself. If being kinder to yourself still feels like a challenge, think about how you would talk to a small child or a close friend, and go from there.

Think back to the first time you felt lonely as a child. You may have been crying and feeling unaccepted or sad. What would you tell that version of yourself? What would have made you feel loved at that time? What did you need to hear? Now is your opportunity to give yourself the comfort, unconditional love, acceptance, and kind words that you needed back then.

I know it can be difficult to stay present, especially if you've spent a lot of time trying to keep yourself distracted so you don't have to hear all those unhealthy thoughts. Give yourself permission to stay present and allow yourself the time to notice your thoughts as an observer, without any guilt, shame, or judgment. You can then begin to work on the thoughts before your feelings and behaviors get affected by them. It takes work, but you'll feel so much more empowered when you get to a point where you realize your healthy thoughts outnumber the unhealthy ones, and that is healing. You can do this! Here are some tools you can use:

Affirmations

Sometimes called "I Am" statements, affirmations are a way to consciously choose encouraging statements that you repeat to yourself in the present tense. They can affirm what you already have or what you desire. You can say, "I am healthy," whether you are feeling great right now or if you are feeling sick and desire to feel better. It is about affirming what we already have and calling into reality what we want.

These affirmations are already within your reach because you are alive, worthy, and deserving of such things.

As you begin to create your affirmations, you have to make sure they make sense for where you are in your healing journey. Try saying them out loud and take note of how you feel when you say them. If saying "I love myself" doesn't feel authentic, try something that feels good to you. Maybe "I am learning to love myself" works better right now instead, or even "I am learning to like myself." You can't receive the benefits of the affirmation if you feel like you are lying to yourself.

Consider the following affirmation examples.

Victoria

In the courtroom, Victoria is changing her thoughts by using the following affirmations before presenting each case before the judge:

- I am a winner.
- I trust myself.
- I am an intelligent woman.
- I am capable of making the right decisions.

Gaby

After returning from her retreat, Gaby begins each morning by looking in the mirror and telling herself:

- I am worthy of having a great life.
- I make time for myself and my passions.
- I accept and love myself unconditionally.
- I give myself permission to ask for help.

Nancy

Taking advantage of what she learned during her mini book study with her stepdaughter, Nancy is implementing the following affirmations after she writes in her gratitude journal each night:

- I am peaceful.
- What I want matters.
- I focus on what I can control.
- I am enough just by being myself.

Use the lines below to create some of your own affirmations. Commit to repeating them to yourself on a regular basis each day, because you are deserving of a great life!

My Affirmations:

_____

_____

_____

_____

Viewpoint

Changing your viewpoint is about consciously choosing to look at something in a different way.

It is important to understand both your perspective and viewpoint because you get to choose the meaning you give to the events in your life. You ultimately have the power to decide whether you are going to let something hurt you or empower you.

Whenever we can't change the environment, we want to change the viewpoint. Let's look at Nancy's example. While she was going to school to become a teacher, she worked evenings in a retail store at the local mall. She didn't like the customer interactions she had to deal with. Most days, she'd drive to the mall filled with unhealthy thoughts after her classes were over.

Oh, it's going to be another day of minimum wage and rude customers.

She couldn't quit the job because the money was helping to pay for school and the hours were flexible, making it easy for her to balance classes, studying, and taking exams while making some money.

Her circumstances couldn't change, but she did have the power to change her viewpoint by thinking, *I am choosing to have a positive attitude. I focus on what I can control when I'm interacting with customers. I am the change I wish to see in the world. I know this is a necessary and temporary job that is helping me pay for school. I will eventually get to leave this job and get to do what I love. When I graduate with my college degree, I'll get to make a difference in children's lives.*

Reframe

Unhealthy thoughts may not go away completely, but you can lessen their frequency by using your awareness and challenging them. When you observe unhealthy thoughts showing up, whether they are about yourself or other people, you have the power to challenge them and reframe them. When challenging an unhealthy thought, you could ask yourself, "Is it healthy for me to continue thinking this?"

If the thought isn't what you want, you can reframe it by changing the words to shift it into something that is true and healthy for you to think about.

When you think an unhealthy thought, your body usually gives you some feedback. You may feel uncomfortable or notice that your chest tightens or your stomach feels upset. Then some guilt or shame may set in, making you feel uncomfortable with yourself for allowing yourself to give the thought space in your mind. Healthy thoughts are the opposite—you feel good, peaceful, and calm. There is a confidence and comfortability about healthy thoughts.

Unhealthy thoughts about other people tend to come from a place of self-judgment. When you see something in other people, it may be a reflection of something you don't like about yourself or something you wish you had.

For example, maybe as a young girl, you were taught to dim your light. Then you see a woman who speaks her mind and is comfortable with herself, and you think, "Ugh. She is so obnoxious and loud. I wish she would just sit down and be quiet for once."

Use the following chart to list some of your most common unhealthy thoughts about yourself or others in the column on the left. For each unhealthy thought, add a way to reframe it in a healthier way in the column on the right.

	Unhealthy Thought	Healthy Reframe
Victoria	This case is stressful. I don't think I can win.	I am prepared, and I am going to give it my best.
	That prosecutor is such a kiss-ass. I wish she'd just die.	Every attorney has their strategies in the courtroom. I don't have to like them, but I will practice being respectful.

Gaby	I am in a miserable marriage. My husband doesn't love me.	I am going to take responsibility for my marriage. I will do what I can to have a healthy relationship.
	The new wife in our church group is so clingy. She needs to keep her hands to herself.	Her love language must be physical touch. It isn't mine, but I can remind myself that she appreciates a hug from time to time.
Nancy	My relationship with my mom is the gold standard I'm incapable of. My stepchildren will never love me.	I love my stepchildren, but I can't control how they feel about me. I will continue to show up for them and be authentic to who I am.
	My stepson is an ungrateful little pig. He never cleans up after himself.	I trust myself to have a calm conversation with my stepson about my expectations when it comes to cleaning up after himself.

You		

Reclaim

You learned about the negative effects of following an unhealthy thought that your brain gives you to fill in the blanks when you don't have all the answers right away. Our minds like certainty, and when something feels unresolved, they often rush in with a story, usually one that's shaped by fear or old wounds. Reclaiming your power means gently stepping out of that spiral. It's choosing a more peaceful stance. It's realizing that you don't have to believe every thought just because it showed up in your mind.

Reclaiming your power looks like taking a pause before reacting. When you feel anxious about a situation or relationship that feels uncertain, slow down. Breathe. Come back to the present moment, the way we talked about earlier: by noticing what you see, hear, and feel right now. Remember, the goal isn't to force the anxiety away. It's to make space for a different kind of response.

This is where the shift happens. Instead of going along with the first painful thought, thank your mind for trying to protect you. Then choose to offer a more grounded, hopeful possibility. You might say, "Maybe this person is just having a hard day," or, "This moment doesn't define my worth." That's how we begin to create an empowering narrative, one that lifts you up instead of keeping you stuck.

Reclaiming isn't about pretending things are perfect. It's about remembering that you get to decide which story you believe. That choice is where your power lies.

Let's check in with our friends and see how they're using some of these tools.

Victoria

Victoria has been working with her therapist to reclaim her power in regard to the abuse that she experienced and the fact that her mother didn't believe her when she had the courage to speak up.

The story she told herself as an adult was, "I was sexually abused, and my mom didn't believe me. Now I live a fake life as a lawyer because I pretend to have it all, but I am damaged. I don't trust anyone, and I'm not trustworthy because I do whatever it takes to win. I sleep around because my body is worthless, and it doesn't really matter what people do to it."

Her new, empowering story is, "I now know everything that happened to me had a purpose. I can learn and heal from my past. It has made me a stronger person. Because this happened to me, I am able to empathize with survivors and understand them in a way that other people cannot. With all the knowledge I have gathered and my resilience, I have the capacity to deal with very difficult situations in family law.

Gaby

Gaby is learning how to shift her self-talk. She recently found herself thinking, *I feel sad. I should host three more dinner parties this month*. She realized being really busy doesn't make her feel happier. It actually makes her feel worse when she overextends herself that way.

She took a deep breath, paused for a moment, and shifted her self-talk to match her worth: *I can find a healthy balance between prioritizing my needs and helping others. In peace, I find joy.*

Instead of planning more dinners, she made an appointment for a solo day at the spa later that week. She is learning that she has to be calm and pour into herself first.

Nancy

Nancy is working on changing her viewpoint. She has begun to learn that her stepchildren respect her more when she doesn't try so hard to be someone she isn't. She understands that building relationships with them like the one she has with her mom will take time and will happen organically. She is learning that she can trust herself, she is enough, and what she does is enough.

Just recently, her husband shared his son's favorite meal, and she made it perfectly. When her stepson came home from baseball practice, she met him in the kitchen and told him dinner was ready. Instead of grabbing a plate from the cabinet, he went to his room for hours. Nancy felt proud of herself for not deciding that her efforts were worthless and instead thinking to herself, *He knows this meal is ready for him whenever he wants it.*

Nancy smiled to herself when she later found out that he had a school project to finish after practice, and he devoured two platefuls later that evening.

I know that working on your thoughts can bring a lot of awareness to where your mind has been over the past years, and it can be painful. Remember to be patient with yourself because thoughts are only one piece of the puzzle.

As you read this chapter, you realized that your thoughts influence how you feel. You deserve to feel joyful and happy! To experience all those comfortable and amazing emotions, your thoughts need to be aligned.

We will be diving deeper into feelings in the next chapter, where we will explore how you can express your feelings and be able to manage them in healthy ways.

Chapter 7

Expressing Your Feelings

The soft sound of birds chirping on her phone's alarm clock becomes more clear as Nancy opens her eyes. After a nice head-to-toe stretch and the affirmation "I am grateful for my body," she reaches over to grab her phone from the nightstand. Once she turns off the alarm, Nancy notices that she missed a call from the principal of her school. Immediately, a wave of anxiety crashes over her. The old familiar tightness starts to spread from her chest up to her throat, and she wonders, "What did I do wrong? Am I getting fired?"

Her feelings of panic and sadness at the thought of losing her job make her hands shake. Her face feels hot and her heart begins to race. She isn't even out of bed, and she is already overwhelmed. Nancy sits the phone back on the nightstand and drops her head onto the pillow as she pulls the covers back over her face, trying to fight back the tears that welled up in her eyes as she hates herself for not conquering this anxiety. As she slows down her breathing, she realizes she doesn't actually know why the principal called her. There's no sign of bad news, and yet her body has responded with an immediate storm of emotions. She decides to take one more deep breath and call him back instead of worrying all through her morning routine and on the drive to school.

We've all experienced moments like this, when our feelings seem to take over and cause us to react before we have more information. It can feel like there is an invisible force inside us that chooses our emotions for us as different situations arise. But there is hope, because healing is within you. You can learn to express and manage your feelings, just like Nancy did when she chose to slow down and make the phone call.

> *Part of your healing journey is to understand that your goal isn't to eliminate certain emotions or feelings.*

You will experience all the feelings that exist at some point in your life. Part of your healing journey is to understand that your goal isn't to eliminate certain emotions or feelings—never feeling stressed, anxious, or overwhelmed—but rather to allow yourself to experience these feelings without judgement and knowing that they will pass.

Remind yourself, "I am human. I'm going to feel these emotions, see how they feel in my body, and allow them to come and leave. I know I don't want to feel like this for the rest of my life, or even for a few more hours. So I'm going to learn the tools to help me express and release these feelings in a healthy way."

All feelings are okay to feel. You are human, and the beauty of being alive is that you get to experience the full spectrum of emotions. In this chapter, we will look at how to identify what you're feeling, how to connect with your body, and how to express your feelings in a healthy way. Our bodies are constantly speaking to us, and if we look at the clues, we can identify exactly what we are feeling.

Patterns

Think of your feelings as an ocean. When storms from the past churn the water, it can be difficult to see what lies beneath the surface. Just like Nancy's fear of losing her job, new storms can often carry echoes of old fears. But as the waves settle, you can begin to navigate with more calm and clarity.

This is why gaining a deeper understanding of your feelings is so important—it helps you learn the difference between authentic or repeated patterns from your past. Your feelings may not be one-hundred-percent your own but a mix of what you observed growing up and what was modeled by the people you grew up with.

Certain feelings can be passed down from generation to generation. Maybe you've struggled with keeping romantic relationships, but as you continue to develop more awareness, you notice a pattern—your grandmother lived through a marriage of abuse and domestic violence. Then her daughter (your mom) was a single mom who never remarried. Those experiences can affect your feelings, causing you to feel sad or unworthy around a partner, scared, or even in disbelief that you can have a healthy relationship with a partner.

You may have thought that your feelings were something that happened to you. You fell and scraped your knee, felt hurt and embarrassed, and cried. Your best friend moved away, and you felt sadness and loneliness. You aced a test, and you felt proud and happy. You may have grown up with your feelings as an outcome from a cause-and-effect relationship like those examples above. However, your feelings are more than just reactions; they are also reflections of how you've been taught to perceive the world around you.

We explored how your thoughts can impact your perceptions and experiences. But how do thoughts and feelings interact? Your feelings are triggered by your thoughts. Thoughts like *I'm unworthy* or *I'm a failure* are likely followed by emotions of shame, sadness, or hopelessness. If you shift toward healthy thoughts, such as, *I'm capable* or *I am deserving of good things*, you will feel more confidence, joy, or peace.

Managing your feelings starts with managing your thoughts. It's important to challenge unhealthy thoughts because they can influence how you are feeling. Feelings come and go, and as they do, you can learn to accept them because they are a part of you.

For example, Nancy's first reaction to her feelings of anxiety used to be, *I hate how anxious I am. I wish I could make it go away.*

But she learned to accept her feelings and understand that however she feels, it is temporary. She now has the self-compassion to remind herself that she can take a moment and make a different choice. Instead of blaming herself for her anxious feelings and adding guilt and shame, she can work through her feelings by expressing them in healthy ways.

We are human, and we are allowed to feel angry from time to time. Anger is not the issue, but what we do with it could become an issue. You can be angry and choose to punch your partner, or you can feel angry and choose to have a conversation. The feeling isn't wrong; it comes with the responsibility of how we express it. Once we have the awareness to identify our feelings and allow our bodies to process and release them, our behavior is going to be different. Maybe you choose to punch a pillow when you feel angry because it won't hurt you or anyone else.

Once you can shift from letting the emotions take over to identifying your feelings, expressing them in a healthy way, and taking responsibility, you'll notice a difference in how supportive and compassionate you can be toward yourself throughout the day.

Nancy's initial fear about her boss's call transformed into calm curiosity once she questioned the thoughts that triggered her anxiety. She took some deep breaths, and when she called the principal back, she found out that her expertise was needed to help a new teacher communicate with upset parents. Feeling proud for managing her emotions, Nancy drove to school with a smile on her face.

Avoidance

When was the last time you allowed yourself to cry? Maybe when you were younger, someone told you, "Go to your room and come back when you are happy," or, "Little girls are always smiling. Come back when you've fixed your attitude!"

If you learned to consciously not accept any of those uncomfortable feelings, you may be frustrated and working hard to suppress the discomfort. If you continue denying your feelings and avoiding them, you are hurting yourself and blocking your healing. On the other hand, you may be avoiding your feelings subconsciously due to the repeated pattern of not accepting them and hiding or masking. That is when you pretend everything is fine or look for ways to distract yourself with sex, alcohol, food, or other unhealthy behaviors.

If you were encouraged to hide your feelings, you might struggle with expressing or even acknowledging them as an adult. If you were given space to feel and talk through your emotions, you might be more in tune with how you're feeling today. The good news is, you can always learn to reshape your relationship with your feelings, regardless of the circumstances you faced in the past.

Uncomfortable feelings like sadness, anger, or fear are part of the human experience. Many of us, however, avoid or suppress these feelings, especially if they remind us of painful past experiences or moments of rejection. When we receive unexpected feedback from others as a result of expressing our emotions, it may cause us to feel unworthy or inadequate and want to hide them.

For example, when you feel angry, do you allow yourself to express it, or do you avoid the feeling and start drinking? Then when the anger comes out after you're drunk, it might seem easier to blame the alcohol instead of taking responsibility for the anger that hasn't been processed.

Failing to recognize your feelings as they arise can build up over time, often becoming bottled up within you. This buildup can lead to moments of emotional overflows when you're no longer in charge of your feelings and they control you instead. Instead of taking conscious steps, you can find yourself reacting to every situation, which can result in being numb, not having empathy for others, or getting angry easily or frustrated because you have too much on your plate. You are like a ticking bomb waiting to explode.

Then when you have so much built up within you, it's going to come out in unhealthy ways.

Maybe you get home from work and scream at your kids. You might think about ending it all and just crashing your car into something. Or maybe you go through life feeling angry at the world, being closed off, and avoiding interactions with others.

Suppressing or avoiding your uncomfortable feelings affects your emotional well-being. When you consistently choose to push down your feelings like anger or sadness, you can actually limit your ability to experience other emotions as well, including those comfortable feelings like joy, happiness, and love.

Your feelings are interconnected, and you are meant to experience the full spectrum of them. Maybe you think you are helping yourself by not expressing these emotions, but you're also punishing yourself and not allowing yourself to feel all the goodness, magic, and joy that you can feel in this life. Expressing your feelings isn't a sign of weakness; it is a reflection of your humanity.

Triggers

Nancy's first year as a teacher was difficult. She got a lot of after-school phone calls from the principal and the assistant principal, telling her what she wasn't doing well and how to improve her lessons and classroom management. She worked hard to create a Pinterest-worthy classroom and an open, welcoming environment for her students. Although she took their advice to heart and worked hard to be her best, she felt like she couldn't do anything right during that time. Their lack of praise for what she did well added to her anxious feelings.

Early in her marriage, her husband would call or text her at lunch and would point out little things he thought she wasn't doing well at home, like leaving her cereal bowl on the counter in her rush to leave the house instead of putting it in the dishwasher.

Over time, whenever the phone rang, she taught herself to brace herself for news of what she did wrong. By identifying that her phone was a trigger, Nancy could slow down and understand that her past events didn't have to control her life in the present. She understood that their comments are feedback that she can accept or not. She now knows that she has the power to reclaim her story. She decided to forgive the principal and all her comments during her first year as a teacher. She learned to be grateful for the experience because it helped her become the great teacher she is today.

Many of the feelings you experience today are rooted in past experiences. The way your parents responded to your feelings, the friendships that shaped your adolescence, and the heartbreaks that left you questioning your self-worth—all these have left emotional imprints on you. If you've ever found yourself reacting strongly to a seemingly small incident, it could be because that moment tapped into an unresolved emotional wound from your past, commonly known as a trigger.

Emotional triggers are situations, words, actions, people, or anything that can set off a strong emotional reaction in you. And it may seem like an overreaction to the actual event when you reflect back on it. Triggers can make you feel like you've lost control over your emotions and send you spiraling into anxiety, sadness, or anger.

You know that every time you go to your aunt's house, you feel anxious and uncomfortable. This weekend you're going there, so that means you need to be aware of how your body reacts. If you notice your hands starting to get sweaty, maybe you can walk away, go to the restroom, and take some deep breaths while you wash your hands instead of waiting until you feel like you want to run away.

When you can plan ahead and notice, you are in charge, and you are not letting your feelings take over. You're going to feel proud as you learn how to manage your emotions.

If you pause to consider why you're reacting this way, you might realize that their comment triggered a deeper feeling of inadequacy that you've carried for years. By identifying the root cause of the reaction, you can begin to respond in a healthier way, like Nancy did when she slowed down and questioned her reaction to the missed call.

When you encounter an emotional trigger, try the following steps:

Pause and breathe. Take a deep breath to ground yourself in the present moment. Notice how your body feels, and allow yourself to experience this feeling in your body for a few minutes.

Name the feeling. What are you experiencing right now? Is it anger, fear, sadness, or something else? Be as specific as possible. This will help you identify other triggers in the future.

Ask yourself why. Why am I feeling this way? Is it because of the situation at hand, or is it connected to something deeper? Be an investigator, and be open to what comes up for you.

Validate the feeling. Remind yourself that it's okay to feel this way. You are human so give yourself some grace.

Choose a response: Decide how you want to respond. Do you need to take a break, set a boundary, or express yourself? Remember that there is nothing wrong with the feeling. We have to take responsibility for how we respond.

The more you practice this, the more grounded and in charge you'll feel to be able to respond with clarity instead of reacting out of habit.

As you continue your healing journey, you will face many triggers. Being triggered doesn't mean you haven't grown or progressed. Be patient with yourself. There will be moments when you realize that a trigger is no longer there after the same situation presents itself. You will also notice new triggers because now you may be ready to process and release the pain point that the trigger activated.

Allow

> *It is about allowing yourself to feel and giving yourself permission to experience life.*

There are moments in life when we feel as if our emotions are controlling us. We've all had moments when we feel we are driven by anger, frustration, or sadness to say or do things that we later regret. In those moments, it's easy to feel overwhelmed or out of control, like you're going to lose your mind. Learning tools to manage your feelings can help you understand that things are going to happen, but you'll be able to release them in a healthy way. It is about allowing yourself to feel and giving yourself permission to experience life. Managing your feelings doesn't mean that you are suppressing or trying to control them in a rigid way. It means taking responsibility for them, acknowledging what you're experiencing, allowing yourself to feel these feelings, and choosing healthy ways to respond.

This means allowing yourself to fully feel, accepting yourself and loving yourself unconditionally through them. It is also being able to release them in a healthy and intentional way.

By pausing to listen to your body and how you're feeling, you allow yourself to experience the frustration or stress rather than masking it. Maybe you notice that you are feeling sad. You can tell yourself, "I'm feeling sad right now. It's okay to feel this way. I'm going to let myself cry. I can release this feeling of sadness in a healthy way. I want to feel peaceful after this release, so I'm going to go for a walk when I finish crying."

Sometimes external things can happen that affect how you feel. Maybe you woke up, meditated for a few minutes, and left your house feeling happy. You interacted with the server at the coffee shop, and you said good morning to the person sitting next to you. Instead of responding, they just glanced at you and looked away. That little interaction can take you back to feeling angry at the person, frustrated, and even doubting yourself. You may even wonder if you're putting on a show and should go back to your old disengaged self.

As interactions like these happen, allow yourself to process the feelings. Realize that them not acknowledging you had nothing to do with you and everything to do with them. So as you continue to heal, be honest with yourself. If you want to smile and greet others, do it! If you feel frustrated, scream in your car or punch a pillow. Then go back to the healing and authentic version of yourself.

Another version of allowing your feelings can look like identifying: "Okay, that made me feel frustrated or angry that this person ignored me when I was having an amazing day and greeted them with a smile. Maybe they're having a bad day. I can send them love and go on with my day. I get to release this anger, and then I am going to choose to go back to feeling amazing because that feels better in my body."

Allowing yourself to feel and release uncomfortable emotions doesn't mean that you are giving up control. It actually means you are accepting responsibility for your emotional experience. You can find balance and won't have to carry the weight of unresolved feelings that may burst out after being pushed down. You'll find yourself having less physical symptoms. When you can recognize your feelings as they arise, feel them fully, and allow them to pass, you will strengthen your emotional clarity and have more peace in your life. When you allow yourself to manage your emotions, you are better able to navigate the ups and downs of life with resilience and inner peace.

> *When you can recognize your feelings as they arise, feel them fully, and allow them to pass, you will strengthen your emotional clarity and have more peace in your life.*

Identify

"How are you?"

"I'm okay. How about you?"

"I'm good."

Sound familiar? We have a lot of feelings to choose from. Many of us grow up avoiding feeling words, often resorting to simple words like "good," "bad," or "okay." Learning to be specific with how we feel can open the door to a deeper, more compassionate understanding of ourselves.

I like to teach my clients how to use a Feelings Wheel. It includes core emotions like happiness, sadness, fear, and anger and branches out to more specific feelings like joy, frustration, or inadequacy.

Instead of saying, "I feel bad," you might tune in to your body and get as specific as possible. Instead of *bad*, you may feel *miserable, inadequate, inferior, insignificant,* or *irritated.* You could also reflect on feeling *good* with feeling *confident, cheerful, amused, proud,* or *thrilled.*

Go as deep as you can to authentically name your feelings. Strengthening your ability to become more specific about your emotions gives you the freedom to fully experience them and move forward in your healing journey. It also allows you to communicate more openly with others.

You can replace responding that you feel "fine" or "not okay," with, "I'm feeling stressed because I'm working on a big project," or "I'm feeling joyful because I accomplished a task I had been putting off." The more you understand your inner world, the more you can connect authentically with yourself and those around you.

I invite you to get familiar with how you are feeling by doing check-ins with yourself throughout the day. Check in with how you are feeling when you wake up, midday, and at the end of the day. Use a Feelings Wheel to be as specific as possible. The more you practice this, the easier it will become.

Notice

It's important to notice how your body is speaking to you to communicate about your feelings. Often, you can identify when you are feeling anxious or stressed if you tune in into your body. Sometimes you may not know how you're feeling, but your body is talking to you. Your body often sends signals when you're experiencing different emotions. Maybe your hands get sweaty. Maybe you can feel your heart beating really fast. Maybe you can't stop shaking your leg. Learning about the signals from your body and what they mean can help you understand yourself even better.

Notice and build the awareness that when your heart begins to race, it could be that you are experiencing feelings of anxiety or excitement. A knot in your stomach could be a signal that you are about to come face-to-face with something you fear.

Many times, we avoid listening to our bodies. We want to say something but choose to ignore the feeling and just push it down, only to feel a knot in our throat. Sometimes we want to smile and jump when our body wants us to express excitement, but we decide to ignore our body cues and choose to tone it down for fear of being judged. Have you made that connection, that not listening to your body and not noticing your feelings is hurting you?

Consider the physical example of a recurring headache. If it happens once, it's easy to forget about after taking some medicine and pushing through the rest of the day. I recently had a headache that just wouldn't go away. After two days of suffering through with a headache that wouldn't go away, I chose to slow down and check in with myself.

I accepted that I was overwhelmed and frustrated. I let myself cry and tune in with my body. When the crying stopped, I said, "Okay, I'm too overwhelmed. What do I need to do to feel better? I want to feel calm and at peace. I want to feel joyful. I don't want to go to that event feeling like I don't want to be there."

I realized it was time to reevaluate my schedule and say no to things that didn't really add to my life. Doing so helped me work through and release my feeling of overwhelm and get some much-needed rest. Once I

> *You deserve to say no and choose yourself. Just listen to your body and learn to understand the way it communicates with you.*

did that, my headache went away. Many times, we push ourselves to talk to people who are toxic or go to the event we are not interested in just to feel depleted after.

You deserve to say no and choose yourself. Just listen to your body and learn to understand the way it communicates with you.

But what happens when you've been ignoring that inner voice for years—when you've pushed past exhaustion, swallowed your truth, or kept showing up for others while abandoning yourself? Over time, those unspoken feelings and unmet needs don't just disappear; they settle into the body.

In *You Can Heal Your Life* by Louise Hay, she talks about how our physical symptoms often reflect emotional wounds we haven't yet processed. A persistent knee pain might not just be about a strain; it could be about feeling unsupported or carrying the weight of everything alone. An upset stomach might be your body's way of telling you that you've been denying your truth or forcing yourself to stay silent when something feels off. When we ignore our body long enough, it doesn't stay quiet. It speaks louder, often through pain. This isn't to blame ourselves but to bring a gentle awareness. Your body is always trying to help you come back to wholeness. Listening to it, honoring it, and learning its language is one of the most powerful ways you can choose yourself.

Whenever you connect with your body, the feelings are going to come out naturally, and it will feel really good as you allow them to come out in a healthy way. It is important to identify how you're feeling and to become so in tune with your body that you know exactly how each feeling feels in your body.

When you are in constant communication with your body, it's easy to identify how you're feeling. Let's give it a scale 0–10, 0 being the feeling is not there and 10 being having a very intense feeling.

You can recognize if you are at a 2/10 for anger instead of a 10/10, because realizing it's at a 2 allows you to pause, take a deep breath, and think about what you want to do next. If you wait to do anything until you are at a 10/10, the feelings will have taken over, and it will take longer for you to come down.

Taking action when you are in that space can make conversations unpleasant because you aren't going to get anywhere. You'll be blaming the other person, pointing fingers, and saying things you may regret later.

Of course, this takes practice. It is difficult to go from living at a 10/10 all the time to recognizing the small clues that your body gives as your feelings move up the scale. Listening to your body and understanding the physical experiences can give you a more compassionate and empathetic relationship with yourself. Noticing and strengthening your emotional awareness can help you respond to your feelings in a healthy and constructive way.

Validate

You are human, and you are allowed to feel any feeling that is coming up for you. You have already numbed, ignored, or suppressed your feelings. Today make the choice to start validating your feelings.

Validating your feelings means being honest with yourself, and being able to say, "Okay, I feel sad. It's okay to feel sad right now. I'm going to release this feeling by crying, screaming, drawing, or journaling. I am going to sit with this feeling for ten to fifteen minutes, and then I'm choosing that I want to feel better, so I will engage in thoughts and behaviors that are aligned with feeling better."

We are just using better as a placeholder, but remember, be specific. How do you want to feel? Calm, happy, grateful? Engage in thoughts and behaviors that will make you feel that way. Say to yourself, "I know I can do something about it with a healthy coping skill. This feeling is temporary, and I know I am capable of managing my feelings."

Validating your feelings is an integral part of your healing journey. It will not only help you, but it will help you build empathy and understanding for the people around you.

Gaby jumped when her son slammed his bedroom door when he got home from school. Instead of getting angry and yelling at him, she chose to validate his feelings and have a conversation with him by saying, "I know you are upset or frustrated with something. It's okay to feel like that sometimes, and I'm here to talk about it whenever you are ready."

The following day, her daughter yelled, "Oh, you hate me! Why are you doing this to me?"

Validating her feelings could be something like, "I know you're upset because you're not allowed to go to the party. It's okay to be upset. You can go to the movies or the mall instead."

As Gaby is learning to allow and validate her own feelings, it is becoming easier for her to do the same with her kids.

Let's review. When working on accepting your feelings, the first step is to identify the feeling. Then validate it by saying, "It's okay to feel like that." Allow yourself to experience that feeling and notice how it feels in your body. Then give yourself permission to release it in a healthy way. Expressing your feelings in a healthy way means that it doesn't hurt you or anyone else.

Sometimes people can get confused and think, *I'm going to express my feelings by cussing that person out because I'm feeling angry, so I just need to say it.*

But that not only hurts the other person, it also hurts you when later you feel regretful or ashamed for what you said. So how can you express your anger without hurting yourself or somebody else? Try going for a run and think about all the anger rushing out of your pores with each stride. Or you put on some music and dance, visualizing the anger leaving your body with each movement.

Embrace

Expressing your feelings is not just about following the steps but about fully immersing into the experience. Embracing your feelings can help you gain insight on how incredibly strong you truly are. Expressing those uncomfortable feelings like vulnerability or disappointment might have once felt like weakness, but now you are learning to see them as a journey to becoming more resilient and accepting yourself fully.

As a child, you may have learned that being sensitive wasn't valued, but as an adult, you can see it as your personal superpower and a way to relate to others and have empathy for them. Noticing those old feelings of self-doubt and choosing to embrace the journey strengthens your self-esteem. By honoring and accepting your emotional experiences, you build inner strength and create harmony in your life.

A tool to help you embrace your feelings is mindfulness, or staying present. Mindfulness allows us to show up fully in our experiences, but without it, we can get stuck replaying small regrets. Imagine trying to work while your mind keeps returning to how you didn't greet an acquaintance at a recent party. You wonder if you should have said hi or if you should apologize now, and you debate reaching out to her instead of getting your work done. This mental tug can signal unresolved feelings or self-criticism.

In such moments, mindfulness offers a way forward. Instead of staying distracted and trapped in guilt, pause and acknowledge the feeling. Forgive yourself by saying, "I acted in a way that wasn't fully mindful, and I release this moment." With this self-compassion, you free yourself to move forward.

Mindfulness also allows you to act with intention. At that same party, rather than being distracted by scanning the room, getting a drink and making sure you greet the host, you could focus on one meaningful interaction at a time. Then when you see your acquaintance, you can stay present with her in a meaningful way.

You are healing, so be patient with yourself. This process can be embraced and celebrated. By pausing and addressing your feelings with kindness, you not only release the distractions that linger in your mind but also prioritize your well-being. It takes strength to acknowledge your emotions, forgive yourself, and choose a healthier response. Embrace this journey and celebrate your progress with the same intensity as you have put yourself down for your mistakes.

Now is the time to move from dismissing your growth to acknowledging and honoring how far you have come. Recognizing this power within yourself allows you to redirect your energy toward living intentionally and joyfully. Celebrate this ability as a reflection of your inner strength and compassion. Healing is within you!

Healing requires a combination of self-compassion and intentional action. First, acknowledge that these feelings have served a purpose—they were trying to protect you or teach you something. Then, gently challenge what no longer serves you. When you can honor your feelings as valuable parts of your experience, you can begin to let go of unhealthy patterns that keep you feeling stuck and slow down your healing.

Let's look at some of the feelings our friends are beginning to see as strengths and how they are embracing who they are.

	Situation	Automatic Feeling	Embracing Who You Are
Victoria	Victoria feels her frustration growing when she gets stuck behind a slow driver on her way to work.	"Everyone around me is stupid and incompetent."	"I am passionate about punctuality, and I will focus on what I can control."
	While watching a movie, she starts to feel sad.	"Ugh, stop being such a weak little bitch."	"It is a strength of mine to have empathy and compassion for others."

Nancy	Nancy feels ashamed that she and her husband had an argument about which drawer he should keep his socks in.	"Why do you always act like such a control freak?"	"I want the best for my family, so I try to create an environment that reflects my caring nature. I am learning that sometimes caring means letting them make their own choices without worrying."
	She feels exhausted from going to bed at midnight looking at the latest trends to connect with her students and improve her lesson plans.	I need to do more. My students will think I'm stupid if I don't know their lingo. I am going to get fired if my lesson plans are not perfect.	"I am enough. I have nothing to prove. I know I am a great teacher, and I care about my students."

| Gaby | Gaby felt rejected after not receiving an invitation to a get-together with her church group. | "It's selfish of me to say no to hosting. This is what I get for not having this gathering at my own house." | "I can't control what other people do. I will use this time for self-care and to do something I love. I show up for others better when I take care of myself first. " |
| | She felt isolated when she didn't join in a conversation about how worn out her friends were. | "Working on myself is making me lose friends. Change is too hard, and I don't even know if it's worth it." | "I am learning to be kind to myself. I trust that I am healing, and part of this journey includes making new friends who are growth-minded." |

You			

Mantras

How is it going? This is a great time to check in with yourself. Are you feeling proud of how far you have come? Overwhelmed of all the healing you think you still have to do? In those moments when you find yourself feeling overwhelmed with your emotions, mantras can be a comforting way to release and process them.

Identifying one thing you can say to yourself over and over can help you come back to your senses, pause, and center yourself. When I felt so overwhelmed with my schedule, the mantra I used was, "When I feel like I cannot take anything else, I can always take in peace."

I repeated it with my eyes closed as I visualized breathing in peace and breathing out overwhelm. I've noticed that when I am overwhelmed, I have shallow breathing, so adding conscious breathing really helps me make sure I am slowing down and being mindful.

Here are a few examples of how our friends have harnessed the power of mantras as they navigate their emotions along their healing journeys:

Victoria:

She often finds herself feeling like she is weak when expressing feelings of sadness. It has been an uphill battle since she was a little girl.

Victoria's mantra became, "It is safe for me to express my sadness. I no longer need to mask it with anger."

This mantra allows her to release her suppressed emotions and embrace vulnerability. As she repeats it, she creates a nurturing space where she can honor herself and her feelings without fear.

Gaby:

After setting boundaries and lessening the amount of social events she hosts, Gaby is noticing feelings of rejection rising up when she isn't invited to events hosted by other church members.

Instead of letting her feelings take over, she remembers to repeat her mantra: "I belong when I love myself, and I am ready to have assertive conversations when needed."

Gaby now trusts herself to have a conversation from a place of curiosity, without breaking down or shutting down, about not being invited and making requests if needed. She has learned that her worth comes from within rather than from the amount of external invitations she receives.

Nancy:

When she struggles with anxiety and notices herself tightening her muscles, Nancy can free herself from pressure and embrace the ebb and flow of being human.

Her mantra became, "I release anything that doesn't serve me, and my body is calm."

It helps her be aware of her body and stretch her neck and shoulders throughout the day. She has also learned to let go of the high expectations for herself and make space for learning experiences.

As you continue to grow, you will face uncomfortable situations that cause you to doubt yourself or your choices, and that is normal. For Gaby, not being invited to a social get-together hurt her because her past of constantly hosting events to fit in wasn't that long ago. Now that she's learning to say no and set boundaries, other people have the opportunity to host. But when she didn't get invited, she started doubting herself, wondering if she was wrong in her choice to put herself first. She considered jumping back into her old pattern of saying yes to everything until she had nothing left to give so she could feel like she belonged.

She allowed herself some time to think before taking action. She pondered on her recently made changes:

I am learning to set boundaries, but then some of my friends don't want to talk to me anymore. I'm learning how to prioritize myself and find my worth within. The people who complain and see life as a tragedy don't think I fit in with them anymore.

She was confused.

Healing is not linear, and it will come with opportunities to choose yourself or go back to old patterns. The choice is yours. What I can tell you is that it is about committing to your healing and being honest with yourself. When in doubt, you can always pause. You are worthy of taking a break and thinking things through before making a decision. You deserve to have healthy relationships, even if it means you have fewer but healthier friendships instead of a lot of superficial ones. Allow yourself to express all the feelings that come up during this process.

Experiencing your feelings is an important part of your healing journey. It's about gently noticing what you're feeling, giving yourself the space to validate those emotions, and finding ways to express them that feel healthy and true to you. Your feelings aren't here to overwhelm you or be ignored; they are here to guide you and help you understand yourself better.

When you take the time to honor your feelings with kindness and release them mindfully, you open the door to more peace, joy, and connection within yourself. Trust that each step you take to embrace your feelings is a beautiful act of self-love and a celebration of your inner strength.

Next, we'll look at adjusting your behaviors to support your growth. Let's continue our healing journey!

Chapter Eight

Aligning Your Behaviors

Each of Gaby's mornings feels a little heavier than the day before as she pulls herself out of bed and shuffles down the hall to get the kids ready for school. Her body moves along as though she's on autopilot—packing lunches, making breakfast, and getting everyone and all their things into the car. Once the kids are handled, she returns to her silent house.

Hours slip by as she sits on the couch, feeling grateful that she has the next episode of her latest favorite show to look forward to. Her alarm signals that it's time to shower and get ready for the school pickup. In the quiet of the shower, Gaby's thoughts become loud enough to hear.

She realizes that she isn't watching television because she particularly likes the shows but because it numbs her and keeps her from facing her true feelings.

"I'm trapped, like a hamster on a wheel, running along and going nowhere. I feel like a single mom when my husband can't give me the support I need. I love my kids, but it feels like I forgot about myself along the way."

She understands that all the shows are acting like a shield. They are an attempt to protect her from the sadness and frustration that she is too afraid to discuss with her husband. Gaby lets herself cry, watching her tears mix with the shower water and flow down the drain. Allowing herself to process the feelings was not fun, but she recognized it as a turning point. It's time to reassess her situation and begin to make the changes that can help her find her way back to feeling more like herself.

As she thinks about it, Gaby also remembers that this is a pattern that has existed since she was a teenager. She was so uncomfortable back then that she remembers cutting her arms and thighs to avoid the emotional discomfort. The cutting gave her a sense of relief because she didn't have to focus on her emotional pain. Rather, she would focus on the physical pain and the burning sensation as she pulled the razor across her skin. She didn't want to kill herself, but she realized that this type of behavior was a way of avoiding her feelings. In the present, it is watching television. Back then, it was cutting.

Now that she has the awareness, she can begin to make a behavior change.

We've talked about the ways your thoughts are influencing your feelings. In this chapter, we're going to explore how our behaviors are also impacting our feelings.

For example, if my behavior is to constantly go for fast food or unhealthy snacks, even though I want to be in a healthy body, of course I'm going to feel ashamed, sad, depressed, not good enough, or overwhelmed. This happens when our behaviors go against what we truly want, think, or say we are going to do.

If I want to feel happy, excited, or peaceful, I not only want to make sure my thoughts are aligned with those feelings, but I also want to make sure my behaviors are aligned with them.

To continue with our food example, that would look like thinking, *I am capable of change. I believe in my determination to prioritize my health. I am worthy of a healthy body.*

The aligned behavior would be reaching for a balanced meal and meal prepping healthy options that are readily available. That congruency will cause you to feel proud and happy about your choices. It is a way to show love to yourself through your behaviors.

Automatic Behaviors

In the same way that we can experience automatic thoughts when we have experienced trauma or difficult circumstances in our past, we can also fall into patterns of automatic behaviors.

After every difficult encounter in court, Victoria goes shopping. This behavior automatically shows up when she struggles with not feeling worthy, good enough, or adequate. In order to feel some relief and regain some sort of self-worth or acceptance, she goes on autopilot. The next thing she knows, she leaves the courtroom and drives to the high-end stores.

As she enters the store, she can feel her posture shift. Spending thousands of dollars on a single designer bag or dress makes her feel important. The associates shower her with compliments on her excellent taste. She soaks in their praise, feeling like she is better, stronger, and more successful than she feels on the inside.

She is beginning to understand that these shopping sprees are a way of getting external validation that is missing from within. It's a different way to numb her feelings of inadequacy. Deep down, she knows that there's more to her worth than what she wears or buys. But that awareness doesn't last. Making lasting change will mean diving deeper and finding validation from within as she works on adjusting her behaviors.

When automatic behaviors go unchecked, they can lead to unhealthy situations over time. Victoria has maxed out several credit cards. It's easy to keep spending when the more she spends, the more compliments she receives. She makes good money, but she is in debt because she is overspending. She feels like she has to hide her debt and just show off all the brands that she's wearing. She pretends to have it all when, in reality, she feels like an impostor and is struggling to pay her credit card bills.

As I mentioned in chapter 5, my automatic behavior for many years was to reach out for food anytime I was uncomfortable. As a young girl, anytime I was sick or sad, I was either given pancakes and chocolate milk, or I would be taken out to eat. I could pick anything I wanted like burgers or tacos. I learned that when I felt uncomfortable or in pain, I could put those feelings on pause and have fun eating something so rich that it would make me forget about those other feelings. That pattern continued for many years.

As I grew up, when I was stressed out, I would automatically want to eat something savory and carb-heavy. When leaving school or work, I would just think about what I could eat that had bread, rice, or was salty and savory. The relief came quickly, but with it also came regret and frustration. I felt ashamed for being an overweight therapist and embarrassed about all the extra pounds I had gained over the years.

This took a lot of healing and awareness. There are many layers to healing this for me. Not just the pattern of behavior of reaching for food when uncomfortable but also learning to love my body. The repercussions from the sexual abuse I experienced looked different throughout the years. But what they had in common is that they caused a disconnect and affected my sense of safety in my own body.

This is something I continue to work on and improve by setting intentions and following through with my behaviors while also giving myself grace. It's about creating awareness and making small changes that can be sustainable. All while loving myself and trusting that healing is within me.

When Gaby realizes that she just binged her way through another series, she feels like her life is passing her by. She feels like she isn't good enough and starts comparing herself to the other women she knows. She took a step back from planning church fellowship events, but she replaced it with television instead of the self-care she needed. It's as though she has a tangled ball of emotions that she carries around with her—all the shame, worry, and sadness that she keeps avoiding.

Instead of disappearing when she sets it down, it just waits for the quiet moments to drop right back onto her shoulders. When she isn't numbing herself, she finds herself joining the gossip sessions with her friends at church and pointing her finger at others instead of addressing her inner pain.

By catching herself after making a comment about someone else that hit a little too close to home, Gaby understands that she can't get rid of those feelings until she is honest with herself. It's uncomfortable, but she's learning that she can start to untangle the heaviness and create a life that feels more aligned with her values and her healing.

Automatic behaviors can occur on a conscious or subconscious level. Consciously, you may think to yourself, *I'm so stressed out. I need to go get a drink*, or *I am too angry and anxious right now, let me go get a pizza.*

Subconscious automatic behaviors can feel like an out-of-body experience. For example, you feel so stressed and overwhelmed with work and lonely when you get home, you feel like you can't find happiness or get a break in your life. So you walk over to the cabinet to pull the vodka, and you just start drinking it without even really thinking about it.

The more you get used to the behavior, the easier it becomes to keep repeating it. No matter how harmless they may seem, all these automatic behaviors can hurt us in the long run. We want to create the awareness to notice them and then make a change to heal.

Self-Harm

Self-harm can come in different forms. The one that most people are aware of is physical injury, which includes any behavior where you intentionally hurt yourself without wanting to end your life. These behaviors include burning, cutting, or hitting yourself. All these to either distract yourself from the emotional pain with some physical pain or to punish yourself.

There is also emotional self-harm. This is when you constantly put yourself down, berate yourself, engage in unhealthy self-talk, and punish yourself emotionally. Many of us engage in this type of self-warm without being aware of it. But now that you are aware, you can choose differently.

Sometimes self-harm can be tied to suicidal ideation. When emotional pain feels unbearable and life seems hopeless, you may feel like leaving this world is the only way to end the pain you feel. This way of thinking can come from feeling misunderstood, overwhelmed by depression, or believing there is no other choice. But as long as you are still here, there is hope for a different life. If you are feeling this way, you are not alone, and there are people who want to help you.

Reach out to a trusted friend, a therapist, or call 988. You can also go to the nearest emergency room or psychiatric hospital for support. Getting the help you need is an act of strength, and it's one of the bravest things you can do for yourself.

Often self-harm comes from a place of guilt, shame, deep sadness, or unprocessed trauma. This can subconsciously make you feel like you need to punish yourself. Maybe you tell yourself you're a bad person, mother, daughter, or friend, and hurting yourself becomes the price you pay for those mistakes. It can be scratching yourself with a sharp object, pulling your hair until you have a bald spot, biting your nails until your cuticles bleed, or overeating to the point of vomiting or just getting sick. Others may self-harm by drinking until they black out.

Self-harm may feel like a release or a way to forget about your emotions, but this is only temporary, and it's delaying your healing. True healing comes from addressing the overwhelming emotions and learning to forgive yourself. You deserve kindness, especially from yourself.

Self-Sabotage

How many times have you tried to make a change? You're really trying your best, but somehow you don't seem to stick to it. Consciously, you are working on improving your behaviors, but subconsciously, you are struggling, and you revert back to your old patterns. The issue may be related to self-sabotage.

How many years have you tried to lose weight? You try to eat healthy and exercise, but it feels like you are going against the current at every turn. At special gatherings, you end up eating the unhealthy food in big quantities because it's only this once. Or maybe you go out to a restaurant and order anything that sounds good because you will start eating healthy the next day.

Months and years go by, and you continue to struggle. Should you continue to want a healthy body, or should you just give in and stay the same? You still have a choice to make. But the healthy choices seem so much harder because it can feel like everything is against you.

This kind of self-sabotage with your diet can have a much deeper reason than just convenience. It may come from being sexually abused when you were younger. Subconsciously, your body is trying to protect itself and not let another rape or abuse happen again. Your subconscious mind feels safer with the extra weight.

What if it is not about the weight but about taking your power back and choosing yourself? When you work on your healing and truly choosing yourself, it becomes easier to let go of what doesn't serve us, including extra weight.

Remember when I told you that this book won't be your last step toward healing? When you apply all the tools in this book, you may see tremendous progress, but some of you may still need more support.

You deserve to have a life that you love.

Because self-sabotage is a subconscious issue, if you continue to struggle, I invite you to address it in therapy or with a professional who can help you. Give yourself the opportunity to be supported. You deserve to have a life that you love.

Caged Awareness

You have developed some awareness, but you are still not breaking the unhealthy patterns. It is like your awareness is caged and you are unable to commit to making a change. You are tired of repeating the same patterns that are not working, and you may be struggling with trusting yourself.

Maybe you don't even believe that you are capable of making a change.

We will talk more about believing in part 3, but for now, know that awareness without change is torture.

So where do we start? Prioritizing yourself.

You've done a lot of work to get to this point! Amazing! I celebrate you and encourage you to feel proud of all the work you have done. I also want to invite you to keep moving forward, but this time with immense self-love to create long-lasting change. You deserve to heal and feel light and free.

Others can be there to support you, but at the end of the day, it has to be you wanting to make that change, wanting to feel better, and wanting to have the best life possible. That means being so committed to yourself that you won't let anything stop you from healing.

You are capable of changing your thoughts, feelings, and behaviors. Prioritize yourself and use the newfound awareness to continue your healing. Now that you know you have the power within you to make a different choice that aligns with the person you want to be, it's time to trust yourself and try new things. You are meant to thrive!

Hidden Resistance

You are working on changing, and it's coming with some frustration because you are still considering what exactly works for you. You have to take an approach that feels right and aligns with who you are becoming. It's a process of trial and error. Trust your path, but if you are not taking action, there may be something deeper that needs your attention. Hidden resistance may be showing up in the following ways:

Shame

You have engaged in this behavior for years. Maybe it's drinking, smoking, overeating, or drowning yourself in your work instead of addressing the discomfort. You are so used to it, and maybe the thoughts that are going through your mind are, *Why change now? I've been doing this for many years.* Or, *It is too hard. I'm already this way, so maybe it's just who I am now.* You have failed before so you end up giving up too soon. Somehow you feel inadequate to make a change and the shame about it prevents you from taking action.

Analysis Paralysis

Maybe you are so overwhelmed that you just freeze. You want to make the change, but somehow you become paralyzed. You have so much on your mind, and just thinking about it is exhausting. The overwhelm makes you feel stuck, and it's hard to take a step forward.

That can look like lying down on your bed and thinking about everything that you have to change: changing the way you talk to yourself and your family, setting boundaries, having healthy meals, moving your body, and improving your spending habits. It's too much that you just feel like you are suffocating, and you end up doing none of it.

Lack of Direction

You may find yourself identifying that you want to make a change, but not knowing where to start. For example, you struggle with constant physical pain. You do a quick internet search and see all kinds of ideas for a first step. You read articles about moving your body to feel better. Another link says you should start by taking supplements. Another says an Ayurvedic doctor is the only way to go. Then come the posts about the pain relief that came when they started working with a chiropractor.

When your head is spinning because you can't find the starting line, you may decide to turn on the television or keep scrolling on your phone. Then hours later, you still don't know what makes sense for you. You just want to feel better, but you don't know where to start. So another day goes by, and you haven't taken a step toward your goal of alleviating your pain. You feel that you need to do more research to know exactly which direction to take, and you continue to not take any action.

Too Many Options

This happens when you have a clear goal but become confused with the number of ways to go about reaching that goal. You know you want to talk to someone so you can begin healing from your past and processing your emotions with a professional. You are ready to start making changes, but you hear about your friend going to one therapist, while another friend goes to a different therapist. Someone else you know tells you about going to a transformational coach or a healing coach, while another person tells you about a major shift that happened for them on a group retreat.

It just feels like there are too many really good options. So where do you start? You find it difficult to trust yourself to make the right decision.

Fear of Rejection

Making lasting changes in your behavior can come with fears and discomfort. Maybe what has stopped you from taking action is fear of rejection. You wonder if your current friends align with the changes you are making or if you're not going to fit in with them anymore.

Maybe they're going to judge you because now you're prioritizing yourself and setting boundaries. You wonder what they're saying when you aren't around: "Oh, she's full of herself," or, "She thinks she's better than us."

All these thoughts cause you to avoid making a change because you are afraid of being rejected by the people around you. Feeling like you won't fit in any longer, you resist change because you don't want to stand out from your family and friends.

Fear of Success

Another way you can stop yourself is being afraid of success on some level. Maybe you fear that you are not worthy of having it all. Perhaps subconsciously, you may feel that if you have it all, that means you can lose it at any point in time.

You get used to those ideas and think, *Why do I deserve to have a peaceful, happy life? Why bother working on what I want if I can lose it all in an instant?*

Then it's easy to go back to what you are used to, because it feels more comfortable and familiar. If you have struggled your whole life, success can feel like some unattainable thing that other people live.

Fear of Judging Others

What is stopping you from taking action could be a fear that if you change and become this better version of yourself, you're going to start judging others, pointing fingers, and finding fault with their behaviors because they haven't changed yet. For example, maybe your family has struggled with money for many generations. You don't know if you want to become wealthy because it could lead to you feeling like you know more than those family members who still struggle. You fear that you may judge them and may criticize their behaviors.

Your unhealthy behavior has become part of your identity and who you are, so it may feel like a betrayal to make a change. Not wanting to look down on someone can feel like a good reason to stay right where you are. Being concerned that a change you make can lead you to thinking of others as less than you is a way to keep you from making changes that will benefit your healing journey.

Taking Action

Now that you have the awareness of what could be stopping you from creating a behavior change, let's talk about how to take action. As you begin to make these changes, it is important to be patient and kind with yourself. It is a process in which there are steps of change that we all go through. Create the awareness of where you are, and keep moving forward.

Mental Preparation

Thinking about change is already a step in the right direction. You are mentally preparing in a calm and peaceful way. You are coming from a place of acceptance, deservedness, and worthiness of a great life. Let's say the change is improving your fitness and running a marathon.

Thinking about running is already a change. Imagine yourself crossing the finish line. Visualize how you will feel on the day you finish your first marathon. Look at what other people did to prepare and notice what resonates with you. Be patient with yourself because even if you're thinking about it and planning it, that is still part of creating the change you want.

When you are paralyzed by Too Many Options or Lack of Direction, take a deep breath and center yourself. After you do the research, trust and believe that you are capable of making a change and move on to the next step.

Planning Ahead

Think of this step as the map you are creating. You will write down the actionable steps you will be taking. Every decision you make is moving you closer to your goal. With your goal of running a marathon in mind, this may involve finding training plans, deciding on a charity to support, or researching different marathon locations.

You're exploring what works for you and laying the foundation for your journey. Then you are going to the store to buy workout clothes and tennis shoes. You're not running the marathon right now, and that is okay because you're still in the planning stage that will have you feeling excited and ready when it's time to act. When your map has been created and you have the basics to start, it's time to move to the following step.

Taking Action

Even though you're in the action stage, you're still trying to find what works for you. That's why it's so important to try different things to see what works. Creating a running plan and doing your research helped you see that you might enjoy running on the beach. Maybe you go to Florida, where you researched and signed up for a marathon. After running the marathon, you realize that you actually like running in the forest better.

You are not going to get to where you want to be unless you're giving yourself the opportunity to try different things. Be patient with yourself. This is going to take time as you move through the steps, but they all lead to the change you want to see in yourself. When resistance shows in Fear of Rejection, Fear of Success, and Fear of Judging Others, remind yourself that you are creating this change for yourself. The right people will cheer you on and will support you. You are deserving of succeeding! Trust that you are a kind and compassionate person because once you get to the top, I know you will pull others to join you there.

Adjusting Gracefully

As you continue to build consistency and momentum, you will have to adjust. For example, if you want to start running and you are able to keep it up for a few months, it's possible that an injury can happen as your body adjusts to the daily movement. Be patient and know that this is not failure but part of the process. We must adapt and adjust during our healing journey.

Celebrate Progress

You have put in the work. You have chosen yourself and have built consistency. Make sure you are taking time and space to celebrate. This step combats the Shame resistance. When you acknowledge your progress, you are building the foundation that sustains your growth. Your efforts are worth honoring and recognizing. The more you embrace your progress and how far you've come, the easier it will become to integrate other changes.

Consistent Change

Creating lasting change is both an act of love and a process of patience. It's about embracing every part of you and nurturing yourself with the belief that you deserve a lighter and softer life. Change takes time, so accept that it will have its ups and downs. What stays consistent is your intention and determination. So let's explore a few options to help you stay consistent.

Replacing a behavior is more effective than trying to leave one behind. For example, if you're used to coping with stress by reaching for comfort food, shifting to healthier options allows you to fulfill the need in a way that more closely aligns with your goals. Instead of mac and cheese or ice cream, you might choose some hummus and carrots or a piece of fruit. Instead of eliminating the action altogether, you can substitute it with something that supports your well-being.

Small steps add up. With Gabby, a gradual shift away from spending hours in front of the television could be to set a timer for an hour. She can still enjoy watching something while creating some space for a new hobby just for herself.

She can begin by thinking to herself, *I am capable of changing. I deserve to work on my passions.*

Then she joins a flower arrangement class where she can meet new people and learn how to make beautiful pieces of floral art to display throughout her home and share with friends. She feels great when she can look at the vase on the mantle in the living room knowing that she created something for herself, by herself.

Adjust as needed. For Victoria, who thinks she feels better when she has external validation through shopping, she may change the amount of money she allows herself to spend each month. Or she could choose to go shopping on the first and fifteenth of each month, giving her a routine to look forward to. Her thoughts would be, *I trust myself. I am worthy no matter what my wardrobe looks like.*

To make her desired behavioral change, she always books a workout class after she leaves the court. Victoria joins the monthly membership for the gym where she takes the class. That means she's committed to making adjustments to stay consistent and get a handle on her spending habits. Even though she's tired and can feel the hint of a migraine on its way, she's still going to make it to the gym.

Instead of going full out with heavy weights for ninety minutes, she just walks on the treadmill for twenty minutes. She is building the discipline to stay committed to choosing herself and improving her finances. So the behavior of going to the gym doesn't change; she just adjusts the intensity or the length of time at the gym.

Lasting change isn't about perfection; it's about progress. It's about honoring where you are and choosing to move forward in your healing journey in ways that feel manageable and kind. With each small step, you are prioritizing your emotional health and building a life that reflects your worth. Celebrate each moment of growth along the way. They are the foundation of the lasting transformation you deserve.

As you continue to embark on creating consistent change, here are other helpful tools:

Awareness

Begin with the gentle act of awareness. This means allowing yourself to recognize behaviors that no longer serve you and exploring the deeper reasons behind them. By asking yourself thoughtful questions like, "What am I avoiding?" or, "What am I hoping to achieve by doing this?" you begin to uncover the emotions and patterns that drive your actions. This understanding is the first step toward healing, because it allows you to approach yourself with compassion instead of judgment. The secret is to come from a place of curiosity.

Awareness helps you see what has worked for you in the past and what hasn't, giving you the space to identify opportunities for growth. Without this insight, change can feel inconsistent or overwhelming. When you take the time to notice and understand your choices, you create space to align your actions with your values and reach your goals. It helps you make shifts that honor your well-being and keep you moving in the direction you want to go.

Discipline

When you move forward with discipline, you let yourself know that you are committed to making the behavior change. No matter how you feel, you're still going to make that behavior change and adjust as needed. Because you are worthy and deserving of choosing yourself and creating lasting change.

I like to talk about three types of discipline with my clients: blind, hate, and love.

Blind discipline is when you set your mind to something and you just do it—no hesitation or excuses. It's impressive, but not very common if you have experienced trauma, and it doesn't always work for everyone.

Hate discipline is when you push yourself to change because you are desperately trying to fix something you don't like about yourself. You may feel broken or damaged and want to fix yourself, fueled by self-hatred. It's hard to feel satisfied, and you may never reach your goal because your motivation comes from a place of self-criticism, anger, and lack.

My favorite type of discipline is love discipline. This is the kind that lasts because it comes from a place of self-love and care. It's about saying, "I deserve better. I want to create a life I love." When you come from a place of love, whether it's working on your health, relationships, or goals, you're more consistent and fulfilled. It's about creating the future you want with kindness and patience, and it's the one I would love to see you working from. You just have to continue to show up for yourself in a loving way.

Love

To see lasting change, come at it from a place of love. Believe that you are worthy of change, and trust yourself to make healthy choices. You will feel proud and inspired when you choose yourself and adjust your behaviors to align with your healing.

For Victoria, that means she believes she's capable of making the change to improve her spending habits. She trusts herself to go to the gym three times per week after she leaves work. The other two days, when she is not booking that gym class, she designates them for self-care. She plans to go home, take a bath, and do something relaxing—maybe a meditation, some yoga, or a mindfulness exercise. She is building the love and discipline to make this change and honor herself as she continues to give her body what it needs every day after work.

Consider the Cost

What is the price you are paying if nothing changes? Begin by considering how much it's costing you to not make this behavior change. Is it your peace, your relationships, your self-esteem, or something else?

For Victoria, if she doesn't change her behavior of going to the mall after work, she will stay in debt. She feels ashamed, like an impostor, and like she's lying to herself. She pretends to have it all but feels empty and inadequate.

Considering the cost of your repeated pattern can give you the motivation to choose differently moving forward. You have paid plenty already. Maybe it has cost you pain and tears. Remind yourself that you are no longer that person and you are not willing to give in to the behavior. Choose to love yourself and affirm that you deserve better.

Notice Your Intention

The intention behind our behaviors matters. Are you happy making this change, or do you feel annoyed by it? The intention and energy we are bringing influences the joy (or lack thereof) during the behavior change and can determine our consistency.

For example, Victoria can book her gym membership with the intention that she is learning to trust herself. She is committed to her physical and financial health. This way, when she goes to the gym, she can stay present and focus on gratitude for her choices and her body while she is working out.

If you go to the gym thinking that you have to because you're fat or you complain to yourself the entire time you're there, it won't become a lasting habit. But you can change the intention behind the behavior by thinking, *I am deserving of having a healthy body. I can enjoy my workouts, and if I don't, I can choose a different way to move my body.* The point is to be grateful for choosing differently and improving your patterns.

Maybe you've been struggling with your relationship with your husband. You're tired of feeling like roommates, and you don't feel like he's being romantic anymore. You ask him to take you to a nice restaurant for dinner, so he does. The behavior is there, but his intention isn't aligned. During dinner, he starts complaining that the food is too expensive.

He says, "This is taking two hours out of my day. I could be working and making more money. I don't know why you want to do this. It's a waste of time. This is worthless."

When he lacks the intention of doing this with love to improve the relationship, it's miserable for both you and him. Next time you work on changing a behavior, center yourself and align your intention. You will find that if you do so, it will be a more enjoyable experience and will make the change more consistent.

Intrinsic Motivation

When you want to make lasting changes, it is important to understand where your motivation is coming from. Is it internal and rooted in your own wants and needs? Or is it external, with a focus on pleasing someone else or meeting societal expectations? While those external motivations may get you started, they don't usually keep you going. Lasting change happens when you shift your focus inward and make it about what you truly want and deserve.

Imagine a single woman trying to lose weight because she wants to attract a partner. Her motivation is external: She's focused on being appealing to someone else rather than loving her own body and working toward her own health and happiness. If she doesn't find a partner, her motivation can fade over time, and her old habits can return because the change wasn't really for her. It's the same with a mother who stops drinking because she sees how it's affecting her daughter. If her motivation is solely about her child and not about her own well-being, she might go back to drinking once her daughter leaves home for college.

Real lasting change comes when you can consciously focus on your internal motivation. Ask yourself, "Why am I doing this? Is this something that I truly want?"

When you can find the answers coming from a place of self-love—because you want a healthy body, a clear mind, or a joyful life—then your motivation becomes unlimited. External reasons can sometimes give you a push in the right direction, but they're not a firm foundation that you can count on. Make sure the change you work toward is about you and for you. You're worth it!

Healing Essentials

I know making a long-lasting change can be difficult. Along the way, you will face situations when things feel too stressful or overwhelming, and you're going to want to give up. When that happens, instead of abandoning your goal, pause and focus on the basics.

When we are feeling too overwhelmed, it's easy to forget about our basic needs. Our Healing Essentials cannot be put on the back burner. This means asking yourself, "Am I drinking enough water? Am I prioritizing my meals and eating healthy foods? Am I moving my body? Am I getting enough sleep?"

Many times you're so stressed out that you forget to eat, or you eat things that are not really nourishing to your body. You may feel compelled to lie on the couch and binge-watch some television like Gaby. Or you may notice that your thoughts of overwhelm are keeping you up at night.

Healing essentials is something that you can use at any point in time, when you're feeling too overwhelmed or like everything seems out of control. You can get a sense of peace by choosing to focus on what you can control. Think back to the Circles of Control exercise we discussed earlier. When many things are on your mind, pause and focus on your basic needs and your body.

Give yourself some time to slow down and take care of your Healing Essentials. This is a necessary focus in your healing journey. Once you manage and prioritize these, it becomes easier to continue breaking unhealthy patterns and making consistent changes. You are capable, and healing is closer than you think!

Practicing Mindfulness

When we are working on behavior changes, mindfulness is a great tool. It improves your self-awareness and keeps you present. You give yourself the opportunity to observe your thoughts and emotions without judgment, which can help you identify the patterns that are keeping you from achieving your desired behavior changes.

Staying present and focused can help you make intentional choices rather than reacting impulsively to situations. Taking a conscious approach not only helps you build up your resilience, but it also creates a solid foundation for lasting change while aligning your actions with your long-term goals. Try the following mindfulness practices:

Progressive Muscle Relaxation

You can quickly release an emotion by squeezing all the muscles in your body as tightly as you possibly can for five seconds, thinking of the uncomfortable feeling being expelled from your body, then releasing the tension for five seconds as you breathe peace into your entire body with your inhale. Repeat the tension and release once again.

Another way to use this technique is by focusing on different muscle groups in your body. Start with the muscles in your feet. Curl your toes under and make your feet as tight as you can. Hold them tightly for a few seconds, then let them completely relax. Continue this process with all the muscles in your body:

- Calf muscles
- Thighs
- Glutes
- Lower back and stomach muscles
- Chest
- Shoulders
- Arms
- Hands
- Neck and face

Meditation

Having a regular meditation practice can help reduce stress, increase self-awareness, and improve your emotional health. Taking time to focus on your breathing can help you notice your thoughts without having to judge them. It can help you learn how to become more present in your daily life.

If you find it difficult to sit with instrumental music and focus on your breathing because it feels like your brain is thinking too much, you can try a guided meditation. That can make meditation easier because you are listening to someone's voice guiding you along instead of feeling frustrated because your brain seems to never shut off. This way, your mind is able to stay present and in the moment.

Journaling

Through journaling, you can create a safe space to explore your thoughts, emotions, and habits in a reflective and nonjudgmental way. This mindfulness practice helps you identify why you do what you do. Writing down your goals and tracking your experiences allows you to stay connected to your intentions and celebrate small victories, which can also boost your motivation to keep moving forward.

Journaling doesn't have to be writing things like "These are all the things that happened today, and it was awful." You can get creative with your journaling. Instead of writing pages and pages, you can sit down and just doodle on the page, use stickers, or create scenes as you are thinking about processing and releasing the events of your day, finding patterns of behavior, and celebrating progress with a feeling of reflection and peacefulness.

Tracking

Sometimes, when we are busy and overwhelmed, it may seem like we are making a lot of progress, but our behaviors might tell a different story. For example, you might believe you're working hard to lose weight or tackle a big project, but if you track your actions—like how often you exercise or the actual hours you spend working on the project—it's easier to see the difference between your intentions and the reality of the situation.

Tracking isn't about judgment. It's about being mindful and honest with yourself. Writing down your actions or timing your efforts helps you see what is happening in real time and gives you the opportunity to make adjustments when necessary. Whether it's committing to thirty minutes of movement a day or focused work on that project, tracking can keep you accountable and clear the noise in your mind. It's a simple but powerful way to align your actions with your goals and create meaningful change.

The way I use this tool is by timing myself. It is easy to get distracted when the whole day I am working on multiple things. I now track my time by timing myself: thirty minutes for gardening, thirty minutes for emails, three hours for clients, thirty-minute break, fifty minutes for marketing. This way, I am being productive and my behaviors align with my priorities in life. I find that because I am being timed, the time I give myself for each task is productive and mindful. It is about quality, not quantity. Try it and see if it helps you stay present and aligned to create consistent behavior changes.

Healthy Communication

Gaby was so used to living for others that she lost her voice along the way. Taking a more passive stance in her life took her down a path of feeling less and less heard, and eventually, she forgot how to speak up for herself. Conversations with her family members were strained, and on the retreat, she learned about healthy and assertive communication.

She used to be aggressive with her husband by saying things like, "You never touch me anymore. Are you not attracted to me?"

"You never look at me. Do you love me?"

"Are you sleeping with someone else?"

But now she was able to take responsibility for her role in the situation and ask for her needs in a way that is more likely to help her get her point across and be heard by saying something like: "I acknowledge that I haven't been my best self. I feel sad that things aren't where I want them to be between us. After going to this retreat, I learned that it's up to me to make some changes. I promised myself that I will take better care of myself and my body. I want to feel more confident and sexy. I'd love for you to notice when I wear makeup and do my hair and let me know that you see me. I am committed to investing in myself and will do my best to communicate with you and the kids in a more productive way. I have a request: Can you please let me know when you find me beautiful or communicate what you appreciate about me?"

When the kids cleaned out the refrigerator, she could say, "Thank you for cleaning out the fridge. Next time, let's work on it together"—instead of her usual comments filled with frustration: "You should have taken all the drawers out and cleaned underneath them. I can see all the spaces you missed, and now I have to do it myself all over again. Thanks for nothing."

Beginning her response with "Thank you" shows her ability to acknowledge their effort. Even though there were ways they could improve in their cleaning, suggesting that they could do it together next time gives Gaby the chance to spend time with them. Helping them learn how to fulfill her expectations without adding feelings of frustration or inadequacy creates a positive experience for all involved.

I have seen this in many women I've worked with, especially when they have a tendency to see themselves as people-pleasers. When they begin to take responsibility for expressing themselves again, passive people who are learning the skills to be assertive can end up jumping into being aggressive. They are not used to being assertive, and it can come out strong.

I attribute this jump from passive to aggressive to a certain level of anxiety. They understand the importance of being more assertive, but the combination of nervousness, practicing a new conversation style, and just wanting the experience to be over can cause a rush of emotions behind the words. Before they know it, the frantic energy creates a level of angry, uncontrollable word vomit. They've been quiet for so long, stifling and holding their true feelings back, that it doesn't feel right and can come out in a reactive rush instead of a productive observation or well-thought-out opinion. So be patient with yourself if you notice this happening to you. It is part of the process as we change this behavior.

Be proud of yourself for speaking up. Celebrate that you are no longer staying quiet and keeping your thoughts to yourself, and know that you are learning a new skill, so it will take time to have it down. Remember that it's okay to slow down and allow yourself to speak your mind in a respectful way that will be received as you intended, rather than rush to say something aggressive and feel guilty and ashamed later for doing so. This way, you can continue with a healthy conversation rather than making the other person feel attacked.

It's a win-win: Your point gets heard, the person you are talking to is more likely to understand you, and you can both collaborate to get to an agreement.

Let's review. When you are ready for an assertive conversation, remember the following components:

- Begin with an "I" statement.
- Communicate what you are feeling.
- Explain why you feel that way.
- Then express your request if there is one.

For example, with Gaby, instead of yelling at her husband and accusing him of cheating, she could say, "I feel frustrated when we don't spend time together. Do you think we could prioritize going on a date night once every two weeks?"

By being willing to talk to him without the added frustrated tone, Gaby's husband can hear her concern, understand why she feels the way she does, and continue the conversation with how he feels. Then they can look at their schedules and figure out which night would work best for their first date night.

I know the example above is an ideal scenario. Sometimes we don't know how the other person is going to respond even if we are communicating effectively. When engaging in healthy communication, your energy and intention is focused on you expressing yourself and not on what the other person is going to say. Let's practice with our other two friends:

Victoria

Victoria texted back and forth with one of the partners in her law firm while standing in line at a café. When she stepped up to order, she noticed an email notification, and she scrolled through its contents as she gave her order to the barista without looking up. She had just enough time to reply to the email before they called her name. Taking a tiny sip, she realized it was the wrong drink.

In the past, Victoria would have slammed the cup onto the counter and growled at the nearest worker through glaring eyes, "How can you work here and be so stupid? I come in here every morning, and I do not understand how you can screw this up."

This time, she took a second to check the name on the cup. It was her drink, but someone must have made a mistake. Instead of demanding their attention, she stood to the side and waited for one of the baristas to set down the next drink.

"Excuse me, I think this chai tea latte accidentally has espresso in it. It tastes bitter to me, and I believe I ordered mine without espresso. I know I was distracted when I ordered, but could you check when you have a second?"

The barista double-checked the order and saw that Victoria didn't ask for espresso in her latte. She apologized, remade the drink, and Victoria was on her way to work. By remaining calm, she was able to get the drink she wanted without losing her temper or stressing herself out over a small mistake that could be easily fixed. Victoria took a long sip of her sweet latte, and a proud little smile formed on her face. *Progress.*

Nancy

During a family game night, Nancy noticed that her stepson kept looking at his phone while she was talking. At one point, she completely stopped talking in the middle of a sentence, and he didn't notice.

In the past, she would have immediately started blaming herself for his lack of attention. Her anxious mind would begin to spiral out of control.

What did I do now? Is he making fun of me to his friends? Why does he hate me so much? I can never do anything right. I don't have what it takes to be a mom.

This time, when she started to feel herself having an emotional reaction, she paused, took a breath, and reached across the table.

Placing her hand lightly on his forearm, she said, "I feel left out when you are on your phone, and I'm trying to have a conversation with you. Do you think we could all put our phones on the kitchen counter while we play the next game?"

She took her phone and placed it on the counter. Her husband and stepdaughter did the same.

Her stepson got up and said, "I just need to respond to the baseball team's group chat first."

After all the phones were on the counter and the next game began, Nancy felt grateful for a distraction-free game night.

Think about an assertive conversation you still get to have. Write it in the lines below. Remember to begin with "I," add a feeling word, explain why you feel that way, and add a request or boundary if needed.

_____

_____

_____

Healthy communication is not only used when we have something uncomfortable to say. We can also use it when we want to acknowledge someone. Assertive communication isn't just a tool for repairing relationships or confronting challenges; it's also a powerful way to build connection, celebrate growth, and give voice to the beauty we see in others. Sometimes we overlook the opportunity to speak up when things are going well, but acknowledging someone's effort, presence, or change can be just as healing as addressing a hurt.

I learned this firsthand with my dad. After thirty years of no communication, we started talking again, and I felt everything all at once. I was hopeful, nervous, grateful, and mistrusting.

I wondered, *Why now? Why didn't he reach out before?*

There was a swirl of emotion in me that I couldn't keep bottled up. So I chose to communicate, not just to confront, but to share.

I told him, "I feel happy that you're finally reaching out to me. I feel hopeful that maybe we can build something. And I feel grateful that you're trying to have a healthy relationship with me. But I also feel confused and frustrated. It's been thirty years, and I need some time. Please be patient with me."

Speaking those words wasn't easy, but it helped me take a step toward healing. Assertive communication, even when layered with emotion, is a gift you give to yourself. It's a way of honoring where you are and what you need, while still leaving the door open for growth.

Boundary Setting

As we are implementing all these changes, you are going to see that the things you were okay with or the people you kept in your circle no longer align with the person you are becoming. Setting boundaries means openly communicating the things you are no longer interested in accepting as part of your life anymore.

Gaby has been working on her boundaries, and as she changes her self-talk, she notices that gossiping with her church friends doesn't feel like the person she wants to be anymore.

At the next gathering, she starts the conversation, "Hey everyone, I'm glad we can have this time together. Let's spend it talking about our goals and dreams, sharing what we envision for the future instead of talking about what we have or haven't liked about certain people at the church."

What she said was respectful, clear, and to the point. Including them with the changes she wants for herself can end up inspiring them to create some healthy changes as well.

If you are on a health journey, a boundary you set with your friends could be something like, "I'd love to catch up, but instead of going to the bar for beer and wings, could we meet in the morning instead for a walk in the park?"

Communicating that certain things are no longer okay because you're changing and it doesn't mean that you are judging them is important when you are setting boundaries. You're just choosing not to engage in the same behaviors from the past because they are not aligned with you anymore.

Instead of crossing your own boundary and meeting your friends at the bar so they stop teasing you and calling you boring, you try a different approach. If it feels safe, you could say something like, "I really don't want to keep going to the bar, but I value our friendship. Let me know when you're ready to meet up somewhere else, or we can have a call and catch up then."

Sometimes boundaries can lead to uncomfortable conversations when people choose not to respect your limits or choose not to listen to you. There may be a time when, due to their inability to accept your boundaries, you can no longer see a relationship with that person. It can be difficult, but in the long run, it's important to remind yourself that your boundaries are in place because they are honoring your true self.

> *You are deserving of amazing and valuable friendships that align with the best version of yourself.*

I understand you can have fears about ending up alone, but be open to the possibility that you are also welcoming new friendships. There is a Mexican saying: *Mas vale sola que mal acompañada*, which translates to "It's better to be alone than in bad company." You are deserving of amazing and valuable friendships that align with the best version of yourself.

Intentional Change

As you continue this journey of healing and choosing yourself, something that can help you with Intentional Change is creating a mantra. Let's expand on what we discussed in chapter 7. A mantra is a short sentence that is going to inspire you or remind you of the reason why you're starting this change. It is about consciously committing to your new behavior.

Here are a few of my favorite mantras when you are working on creating lasting changes in your present to pave the way for a brighter future:

- "I choose to forgive myself, and I know I am capable of making healthy changes because I am worthy and deserving of a great life."
- "I am able to change, and I prioritize my healthy habits."
- "I am deserving of change. I trust myself, and I am learning to listen to my body."

Once you create your mantra, memorize it and repeat it daily. Use it to center yourself, and post it anywhere where it can stay visible, like your calendar or your planner. You can also create phone and computer screensavers with it. Another idea is to use it to create a vision board, which we will discuss in detail in Part 3.

Congratulations, you made it through the "Present" section where we dived into thoughts, feelings, and behaviors. Working with your thoughts is addressing your mind. It's about relearning how to think and work together with your mind so you can have an amazing life. Working with your feelings is getting in tune with your heart. It's about understanding where your feelings come from and how to lean in and accept them. The goal is to become friends with your heart and to trust it.

Working with your behaviors is addressing your body and how you choose to use it. It's creating an intention and clear path to move forward. You now understand how your mind, heart, and body work together, and you are able to make healthy choices. All three of them have to align and be connected for you to have true and lasting change. Working on only one at a time can make it easier to go back to your old ways or have inconsistent change. Remember, healing is within you, and when you can address your thoughts, feelings, and behaviors, you can create long-lasting change.

Now that you've learned how to make big changes in the present, it's time to think about your future! In the next section, we're going to look at the possibilities. You are worthy of having an incredible life, and we are going to get more specific on goals and how to make them achievable.

You will have the opportunity to visualize the amazing future that you deserve while creating goals and actionable steps to get you there. We'll talk about how believing in yourself is essential and how the people around you can influence your healing. Finally, we'll look at ways you can prepare yourself to receive your amazing life and how this is playing a part in the healing of our world.

Let It Be

Let your heart and brain unite
Let your mind and body feel
As water goes down the stream
So may your feelings be expressed and released

You and me can weep and feel
As we remind ourselves that patience and kindness
can set us free
Even when the night seems dark and long
We can look in the mirror and find hope

Let this be the song I sing
When I feel lost and want to flee:
"I got this, I'm powerful, I can learn from this
I breathe, I believe, with faith I ask so I shall receive"

Yes, this is it, I accept who in the mirror I see
The beauty, the scars, and all in between
Step by step, I'm growing and finding peace
I'm healing from the trauma that once felt too deep

This I pray for now and then
To remember to feel and let it be
Here and there, wild and free
I manage my thoughts to build the life I want to live

This I say on repeat:
"There is magic in me to myself forgive
I welcome the lesson, I trust, I let it be
I can learn to completely love and fully live"

I now experience more joy, harmony, wonder, belief
And this I want to always feel
I am getting better at letting it be
I heal, I thrive, I believe in me.

—Carla Calderas

This is what a healed life looks like to me. Accepting that our experiences are part of the human journey. So it's not about suppressing and forgetting our trauma but about living fully despite it all. I am now able to tap into Letting It Be more and more every day. My hope is that you get there too. It is possible to heal from all the struggles and pain. I believe in you! Healing is within you!

PART THREE

THE
FUTURE

Chapter Nine

Our Amazing Future Awaits

I sit down to begin this section that will help you consider your beautiful future, and I freeze. I feel stuck. Everything I do with my clients as a therapist happens in the present. That's what I'm teaching—assertive communication, boundaries—that is where my time is spent. I have all these systems and routines in place.

But how can I write you this love letter for your future when I can't see my own future clearly all the time? There are certain times in my life when I can tap into my future—on vacation, when I'm journaling or during a meditation—but I'm not there all the time.

Sometimes I feel like a little fairy trapped in a mason jar. It's hard to see that there is no lid holding me there. I am stuck, and it seems almost impossible to fly and take myself out of this perceived enclosure. Other times, I can use my wings to get out. That is when I have all these incredible ideas and possibilities about my future beyond the jar. My soul is soaring, and I am filled with the hope of everything that is possible for me. I understand the struggle and know how difficult it can be to think of a future beyond the mason jar.

After all these years of working on healing myself and helping others heal, it is still challenging to see my future clearly all the time. I've been doing a lot of crying and not much writing as I process my thoughts and feelings.

Doubt begins to creep in and automatic thoughts overwhelm me.

Am I lying? Is it even possible for my readers to get there if I'm not there all the time? Is it going to be way too difficult for people on a healing journey to see the possibility of an amazing future for themselves? Is it credible for me to offer this advice while I am still working on it myself?

Then I realize that this is exactly what you need to hear as we get ready to work through this Future section. I'm still learning and growing as I consider my own future. If you find yourself struggling to see your future right now, trust that every step in your healing journey is leading you to the amazing future you are meant to live. Trust your inner wisdom—maybe you call it your future self, your higher self, your best self, or your intuition. This wisdom has more knowledge and awareness than you do at this moment, and you can access it when you are centered. Let's move forward and look at your future by embracing possibility.

Your future holds the promise of incredible transformation through small, intentional steps. Together we will learn to dream, plan, and actively shape the life you want to live while being mindful that your future begins with what you do today.

Back when I was in college, I was majoring in international business and on a path that just didn't feel right at the time. I decided to take a semester off. Something inside of me felt like it was an easy choice to make.

My mom didn't understand why I would take a semester off. She worked so hard as a single mom for me to go to college. She tried to urge me to just stay and finish, but the pain of staying in something that no longer made sense to me would be worse than letting her know I needed time to figure out a new plan. I knew deep down that it wasn't resonating with me, so I chose to honor my feelings. I made the decision to pause, take a semester off, and figure out what really mattered to me.

When choosing between two different paths for your future, it can feel like both decisions have the potential to turn out badly. If I stayed, I could have ended up resenting myself or maybe even my mom for pushing me into something I wasn't interested in or just didn't care for at the time. You may feel like you're just making a decision to please someone else.

On the other hand, it's also difficult to feel like making a desired decision will disappoint someone else. Taking a semester off could have been seen as selfish by others or even hurtful for my mom because she worked multiple jobs to help me through college. The most important thing to do in these cases is to think about what truly resonates and aligns with you. It's about finding the balance between honoring your present and staying connected to your long-term vision.

It wasn't all butterflies and roses during this time in my life. My mom would call me a few times per week, crying and asking what I was doing with my life. It was difficult to try and address her concerns when I didn't fully have the answers myself. Every decision comes with its challenges. It comes down to choosing which challenges you're willing to grow through.

It's important to remember that we need to be kind to ourselves, staying open to new opportunities and ways to connect with ourselves. It could be spending time in nature, walking, or biking. Sometimes it's going to be talking to different people and just seeing what you're interested in.

I gave myself permission to explore different options. I joined a band and was singing. I also tapped into modeling. During that time, I spent a lot of my days walking and biking in the beautiful North Carolina weather. Being alone in nature gave me the space to center myself and ask big questions: "Where do I see myself later on?" "What kind of life do I want to live?" "What do I want my future to look like?" "What are my values, and what matters to me the most?" "How can I live that every single day?"

Through that reflective pause, I began reconnecting with my natural strengths and passions. I remembered how much I enjoyed listening to people and learning from them, noticing patterns in their stories, and offering a different perspective. Even as a kid, I was the one others came to when they needed support. That was when it became crystal clear to me: I wanted to be a psychotherapist.

I knew I had to be strategic about how I pursued my goal. I couldn't afford to major in psychology and then go right into graduate school after that. So I majored in education, which allowed me to work as a teacher while having some flexibility to get a master's degree in professional counseling. It was a big commitment to teach during the day while taking evening classes and using my summers to further my studies, but it helped my earlier vision become a reality.

What I learned during that time in my life was that dreaming about your future is an important step in any healing journey. Give yourself the time to pause and reflect on what truly makes your heart sing. It's not just about the big-picture goals but also the small details, like how you want to feel in the morning, the kind of work-life balance you want, or even the kind of car you'll drive. For me, taking that pause and mapping out the steps was what made my hopes and dreams become the reality I live now.

As we move into the Future section, we will work on three main steps toward achieving your amazing future: visualizing, believing, and receiving.

Visualization has been one of my most powerful tools in shaping my future. I've had a dream of having a space for people to gather for healing retreats. We bought land a few years ago where we could build the space. A few months ago, I did a meditation exercise where I imagined my future self. In this vision, I saw myself in a small cottage in the woods, surrounded by peace and nature. That exercise helped me gain clarity—not just about the big dream of owning land and building a retreat space, but about which step needed to come first. Before I can think about creating a spa center or hosting retreats, I now know my cottage has to come first. That's the power of visualization: It helps you see the possibilities ahead and clarify the next step you can take.

Belief can be fragile. It's easy to let doubts creep in, especially when your circumstances seem to work against you. People around you can also play a role in affecting your belief if you let them. There may be moments along the way when you question whether your dream for your future is possible, and that is completely normal. Belief may grow slowly, and sometimes you will have to move forward even when doubt walks beside you.

Surround yourself with people and experiences who believe in you even when you're uncertain. Curate what you consume—whether it's the music you listen to, the books you read, or the conversations you engage in. These choices matter because they can reinforce your ability to believe in what is possible. When setbacks happen, remember that they are part of the process. It is about persevering through the challenges. We aim for progress and not perfection.

Receiving is our final piece for living your amazing future. Learning to receive is about recognizing your worth and allowing yourself to enjoy the healing journey as it evolves and shifts. That is the beauty of working on your future—your vision can evolve as you grow. Each step forward brings new clarity and opportunities you may have not considered before.

> *Curate what you consume— whether it's the music you listen to, the books you read, or the conversations you engage in.*

Receiving is about being fully present and celebrating what is here while staying open to what's next. Just because we're receiving doesn't mean we sit still. Often, we're invited to move before we have all the answers. That's where trust comes in. When we begin to take steps forward, even without knowing every detail, new paths start to reveal themselves. That's how it was for me. I knew I wanted to be my own boss and build a practice that reflected my values, but I didn't know how to manage a business or lead a team of therapists. I just followed what felt aligned, and the rest began to unfold.

I also think back to my time teaching. I had so much fun with my students. I'd sing with them, pour into them, and show up as my full, authentic self. And because they felt safe and seen, they thrived. They respected the space, and they learned with joy and freedom. That experience reminded me of how powerful it is when we show up in love, not just for others, but for ourselves. It's what happens when we believe in what we're creating and visualize the life we want.

> *In action, we find clarity.*

In action, we find clarity. All it takes is for you to get started. As you get started and work on your goals and your future, you will obtain clarity about the next step to take.

You might not be able to see your future right now, and that is okay. All I am asking of you is that you look at this section with an open mind. If you feel like a specific tool or strategy resonates with you, try it for yourself. If it doesn't work for you, continue reading and try another until you find one that does.

As you grow, improve, and feel better about the possibilities for your future, different tools and ideas will stand out to you more than others. This is a book that you can come back to as you continue to discover that healing is within you.

As you have heard throughout this book, healing is a journey that doesn't stop. We are constantly finding new things about ourselves. There will be setbacks and situations that pop up, but keep reminding yourself that you now have tools that will help you keep working through them. There are different avenues to your healing, and each new path brings its own celebrations and challenges.

In the following chapters, we'll explore practical strategies for setting goals, staying aligned with your values, and creating the steps toward creating the future you deserve. Remember, it's not about perfection, having all the answers all the time, or rushing to a finish line. It's about giving yourself the grace to grow, evolve, and build a future that feels authentic to you. Let's build our amazing future together!

Chapter Ten

Visualize

Victoria has done so much work with the support of her therapist. She's recognizing her patterns. She understands that when she has a bad day at work, she can go to the gym to work on her physical strength and release her emotions instead of falling further into debt.

She embraces that healing is a way of living. Although she isn't completely debt-free, she's only going on a shopping spree once per month instead of a few days each week. She also set up automatic payments so that each time she gets a paycheck, a portion of it goes right to the credit card she's paying off. When she has a setback, she can use her tools and strategies to take a pause and understand why uncomfortable feelings or unhealthy thoughts show up, then she can take responsibility and shift much quicker.

Victoria has now started visualizing her future. It may require a short meditation or some journaling for her to see the possibilities of the amazing life she deserves, but she's willing to take the time to create the routines to help her get there. As she taps into the Victoria of the future, she sees herself smiling. Her presence is filled with a subtle power based on self-love and self-acceptance. She feels appreciation for her body and treats it like a temple. She can clearly see that she is deserving of having all her needs and wants met. There is an inner knowing that peace and abundance are her reality.

After seeing the possibilities for her future, she begins to backtrack and think about what she needs to put in place to make that visualization come true.

She asks herself, "What affirmations do I have to say to make that vision happen? What goals do I need to set, and what is the first step I can take to make this vision my reality?"

Of course, she continues to celebrate the wins as she follows through with the plans she made to change her thoughts, feelings, and behaviors along the way.

For her to be able to let go of trying to control everything and surrender to these new possibilities, Victoria keeps working with her therapist to learn how to forgive herself for everything that happened in her life. She is learning to forgive herself for things that she did and didn't do when she felt powerless.

In this chapter, we'll look at some tools you can use to visualize your amazing future and create actionable steps to help you get there. We will also explore how to stay consistent when your amazing future feels unreachable.

Creating a Vision Board

A vision board is more than just a collage of pictures and words. It's a way to access your future and bring it into reality. It's about gaining the clarity to start moving toward the future you want, step by step, and having a visual to help you get there.

First, we want to center ourselves with a meditation or mindful activity, then we start creating our vision board. Once we tap into the possibilities for our future, we set actionable steps to help us get there.

For me, creating a vision board is about listening and trusting what you feel called to put on the page and, at the same time, being in tune with your life's mission so that it becomes the foundation for your vision board. This can be an exciting activity to do! The beautiful thing is, you're not just thinking about your future during meditations or when you're in a certain space—you're seeing it all the time. The pictures, cutouts, and words are there to remind you every day of what's possible. They keep you focused, connected, and moving forward. The vision is yours, and if you can see it, you can create it and bring it into reality.

To create your vision board, gather magazines, photos, or printouts that align with the future you desire. Create a calming and sacred space where you can work uninterrupted. Next, spend some time centering yourself with peaceful music, a short meditation, or being in silence. See the possibilities and listen to what comes up. Then we get to creating your aligned vision board. Choose images, words, or phrases that spark joy and represent the life you want to live. Arrange them thoughtfully, allowing space for your vision to breathe and expand. As you do this, focus on how these images make you feel, and let that emotional connection guide you.

Vision boards aren't just about collecting pretty pictures; they are a way to envision our future and bring that vision into existence. They are a way to connect deeply with what truly matters to us.

Once you have your vision board, ask yourself, "Okay, how do I get there?"

> Remember that we have to align our thoughts, feelings, and behaviors to achieve our goals.

That's when you start making moves, setting goals, and aligning your actions with the life you see for yourself. Backtrack and create actionable steps that you can focus on daily to bring your future into the present. Remember that we have to align our thoughts, feelings, and behaviors to achieve our goals. We will explore this further later in this chapter.

Let's look at the way our friends created their vision boards and how they are using them to achieve the goals that will take them to the future they desire.

Victoria

Victoria's vision board is centered on love—not just in a new future relationship, but also in her relationship with herself. In the middle, she has a heart surrounding the words "I love you." She chose this message to represent her self-compassion and self-acceptance. She included images of couples holding hands on a beach, symbolizing her dream of a fulfilling romantic partnership. An image of women walking arm in arm represents friendship and belonging. Her dream of becoming financially free shows up as dollar signs and the words "financial freedom." Her final set of images includes women working out at a gym and jogging along the beach. Seeing this helps her believe that she is deserving of friends surrounding her and loving her.

Victoria's vision board symbolizes her desire for love and stability, reinforcing her journey to self-acceptance and the realization that she belongs. She sees herself living a life where she has the mental and emotional capacity to love herself so deeply that she no longer has to rely on external validation or buying material possessions to feel good enough. Her future is about unlimited and unconditional love.

Victoria's goals:

- Lean into her feminine energy.
- Practice trust, especially in herself and others.
- Notice when she feels attraction or connection to someone.
- Engage in more eye contact and allow herself to smile with openness.
- Reconnect with people who have supported her in the past.
- Be more mindful when meeting new people.
- Ask thoughtful questions to discern alignment and potential for genuine friendship.

Nancy

Nancy's vision board contains affirmations like "I am enough" and "I am peace." She included images of a cozy nook with books, a candle, and a warm cup of tea to represent moments of stillness and self-care. A classroom full of smiling, engaged students symbolizes her love of teaching and having a fulfilling career. An image of a woman standing in a powerful pose is a reflection of her growing self-confidence and self-worth. Looking at it makes her feel complete. Every time she looks at it, she is able to access the feeling of being whole as she is.

Nancy's vision board reminds her that it is okay to be unsure about certain aspects of her life and that focusing on herself will bring the clarity and peace she is worthy of. She understands that she no longer has to wait for the approval of others. What she does is enough. The love she has for her students translates into everything she does. There is no longer a need to feel that she is lacking. She can let go of the role of an overachiever and celebrate all the growth that she has had. She is learning to trust herself and affirm that she is enough.

Nancy's goals:

- Be consistent in celebrating her growth and progress.
- Do something kind and joyful for herself every weekend to honor the amazing woman she is.
- Say empowering affirmations three times a day (morning, lunchtime, and before bed).
- Ground herself in the belief that she is worthy.
- Mirror the energy from the image of the woman in the powerful pose.

Gaby

Gaby's vision board encompasses the importance of choosing happiness and nourishing her soul. At the center is the silhouette of a couple in an embrace, with the husband's hand stroking her hair as the other one is around her waist, pulling her closer. She included images of self-care, like spa retreats, journals, and hands reaching to receive gifts to remind her to embrace the joy of letting others care for her.

Words like "ease" and "receiving" symbolize her journey of being in flow and letting others pour into her.

Gaby's vision board emphasizes leaning into her femininity and allowing herself to be loved, to receive, and lean into happiness. She is learning that it is safe for her to be sexy and happy. She is practicing letting go of what others might think of her or their expectations. Her vision board is helping her be herself and accept that she doesn't have anything to prove.

Gaby's goals:

- Prioritize herself by doing one soul-nourishing activity per month.
    - Ask for help from her husband, mom, or church community to manage household responsibilities or kid-related tasks.
    - Set aside time to do something that brings her joy.
- Strengthen her relationship with her husband by focusing on what is within her control.
    - Practice open, assertive communication.
    - Clearly express her needs from a place of self-worth and confidence.
    - Trust that showing up with love and honesty means she is doing her part.

Embodying Your Future Self

What if you can bridge the gap between where you are and where you want to be by embodying your future self? We start with future self visualization. This is a powerful tool to help you embody your future self. Visualization is your opportunity to dream without limitations and use your imagination to access a life where you are healed. Instead of holding back, it's about opening your heart to allow yourself the space to see the amazing future that awaits you.

> *Visualization is your opportunity to dream without limitations and use your imagination to access a life where you are healed.*

What would your ideal life look like if nothing were holding you back? Imagine waking up in the morning begins with mindfulness, maybe sitting in a cozy spot in nature, surrounded by peace. You feel vibrant. Your body is strong from years of loving care, and you move through the day with clarity and intention. Future self visualization is about seeing this with clarity in your mind. Embodying your future self is about connecting with the version of you who has fully embraced joy and abundance—a version you can start aligning with right now.

Embodying means that you are now going to start living from that healed place. You speak with the ease and confidence your future self would. You carry yourself with

> *Embodying your future self is about connecting with the version of you who has fully embraced joy and abundance—a version you can start aligning with right now.*

peace and joy, even on the hard days. It's about practicing in the now to arrive in the future you see.

If visualizing feels challenging, you are not alone. Sometimes life's difficulties make it hard to see beyond the present. When it happens, I encourage you to reflect on your past. Think about moments when you felt joy, peace, or connection. These positive memories can guide you. What moments in your life brought you a sense of fulfillment or passion?

Use those as clues to imagine a future filled with that same spark.

For example, one of my happiest and earliest childhood memories is singing in my driveway, pretending to be a diva with a hairbrush as my microphone. Singing still brings me joy today, reminding me of the pure freedom I felt as a child. As I mentioned earlier, riding my bike in North Carolina and feeling the crisp air on my face gave me deep peace as I experienced nature.

I invite you to explore all the qualities, behaviors, thoughts, and feelings that your future self experiences. Ask yourself, "What would the healed version of me do at this moment?" Choose that, and know that every time you choose to speak or act like her, you become her. Embodying your future self makes healing become real.

Creating with Direction

Now that we've used a vision board to create a clear picture of our future and we're embodying our future self, it's time to create with direction by setting aligned goals. To set goals, we are going to use our vision as an anchor. A vision is a clear, heart-centered picture of the life you are creating. Think of the energy, the feelings, and the clear direction that is guiding your healing. The key is to focus on the future with certainty—knowing that what we see for ourselves is possible and will happen. It's about small, grounded steps that are in alignment with your amazing future.

When we set goals, we don't set them randomly—we align them with our thoughts, feelings, and behaviors. That way, every part of us is working toward our vision.

Part of my vision has been to be financially independent. When I was younger, my mom didn't have a car. We lived in Mexico, and I remember riding the public bus with her. I was exhausted from the heat and always alert to get off at the right time and not lose sight of her.

Back then, having a car of our own didn't just mean a different means of transportation; it meant air-conditioning instead of sweating through long rides with strangers. It meant the safety of being able to go to the store late at night without having to wait until the next day. It was the freedom of going to the hospital in the middle of the night with an ear infection instead of waking up a neighbor to ask for a ride.

So when I dreamed about one day seeing my mom pull up to my school in a brand-new car, it wasn't just about the car. That vision has stayed with me, and when I began working toward financial independence, it was never just about the money. It was a way for that little girl sweating on the bus to experience relief, stability, and the hope that life could feel lighter.

I believed it was possible for me to have a new and beautiful car of my own one day. When I finally bought my first car with my mom's help, it was used—about five or six years old. But in my mind, I knew it was temporary. I had no doubt that my next car would be better. It would be amazing!

My thoughts were clear: I believed that a new car was coming. My feelings were of gratitude for my current car instead of frustration. I didn't hate my car because it was old; I was grateful for it because it was taking me where I needed to go while I worked toward something better. My behaviors backed it up: I kept working, budgeting, and saving because I knew the down payment for my next car was coming.

Then, in 2014, I bought my dream car—a Cadillac CTS coupe, exactly what I had envisioned. I had embodied having that car. I had seen myself driving that car, feeling the excitement of sitting on the leather seats, and believed it was within my reality to have it. That's the process: Align your thoughts, feelings, and behaviors with your vision, and keep moving forward with certainty. Because if you can see it, feel it, and you're putting in the work, it's only a matter of time before the future you desire is yours.

This isn't about perfection or rigid goal-setting. Instead, it's about creating small, meaningful steps that feel achievable and inspiring. Maybe your vision includes being full of energy and living a vibrant life. If it feels overwhelming to think about making so many lifestyle changes all at once, start small. Maybe it's packing your lunch a few days each week instead of grabbing fast food every day. One small win after the next can build momentum, and before you know it, they can lead to bigger shifts.

I know that thinking about goals can feel overwhelming when you don't even know where to start. Sometimes we zero in on just one area—like finances or finding a partner—and put all our energy there. A healed life means looking at all the areas that matter to us—physical, emotional, financial, and beyond. Maybe at the start, you focus on one or two areas at a time while building awareness in the other areas. But as you continue your healing journey, you will notice that your capacity and energy to work on multiple areas of your life at the same time increases.

This is an activity I love to work on with my clients. Once they've made progress on their emotional well-being, I like to check in and say, "Okay, how do you feel about your finances? How are your relationships?"

Healing is not just emotional, so I want to make sure they're in a good place in every area of their life. One way to do this is by using a simple tool like a pie chart to organize life into five sections: physical, mental, emotional, social, and financial.

The Physical section is about your body—how it feels, what it can do, and how you currently feel about your shape, energy, and physical health. The Mental section is anything that makes you feel mentally awake and challenged. It reflects whether your mind feels stimulated and engaged, through work, learning, or creative pursuits. The Emotional section is about how you've been feeling lately, how you're processing life internally, and the overall tone of your emotional world. The Social section centers on all your relationships and whether you feel connected, supported, or isolated. The Financial section represents how you feel about your finances right now. It includes your sense of stability, security, and confidence in meeting your needs. Each section gives you a snapshot of your inner and outer world so you can set focused, realistic goals that align with the life you want to create.

In each section, there are three lines, one each for reflection, intention, and action. The first line is for where you are right now. The second line is your end goal, and the third is your next small, concrete step to get there.

This exercise isn't about fixing everything overnight—it's about checking in with yourself and making small, intentional moves toward the life you really want. It gives your vision shape, structure, and direction.

For example, in my Emotional section, I wrote the following:

- *Current:* I am overweight and often feel uncomfortable in my body, like I'm not good enough.
- *Goal:* I want to feel confident, strong, and comfortable in my own skin. To me, the goal isn't about the number; it's about believing that healing is possible.
- *Next step:* I'm cooking my meals six days a week to feel more in control and grounded.

In Nancy's Physical section, she wrote:

- *Current:* She experiences chronic lower back pain and often wonders if she can trust her body.
- *Goal:* She wants to feel free in her body, to move without pain and reclaim her strength.
- *Next step:* She's committing to moving her body gently for ten minutes every day.

What I love about this activity is that it invites us to reflect and then respond with grace and action. Use the graphic below to get started. Remember, you don't need to map out everything all at once. Just pick a few areas, and give yourself permission to grow, one step at a time.

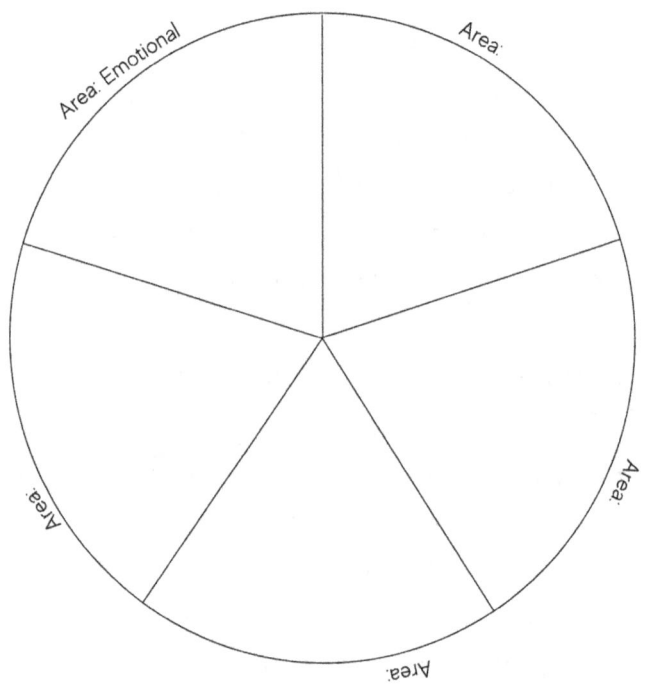

Awakening the Wisdom Within

Your inner wisdom can be your greatest guide on this journey. The answers we seek are already within us—we just need to tune in and listen. Pay attention to your intuition. It's your body's way of guiding you toward growth and alignment. Take a moment to breathe deeply and ask yourself, "What do I need to know at this moment?" Notice what comes to mind and where you feel it in your body. Trust that what comes to you is exactly what you need. Trust the signs that you see. Stay present, and trust that you are being guided.

Anchoring yourself with a meaningful symbol can also help. For me, it's unicorns—they remind me of magic, childlike wonder, and inner peace. Consider a symbol that speaks to your higher self, and use it to stay grounded in times of stress. You have infinite wisdom within you; you just have to access it. As you trust that healing is within you, you will open up the channels for this wisdom to come through.

Treasures for Inspiration

If at any point during this visualizing journey, you feel stuck or need encouragement, here's a tool. A Treasure Box is a beautiful way to keep yourself motivated and inspired. You could use something as simple as a shoe box. Decorate it however you like, and fill it with items that uplift you— birthday cards, notes from loved ones, photographs, or small mementos.

When life feels heavy, open your Treasure Box and get inspired again. Let those tokens of love and compassion remind you of your worth and all the possibilities ahead of you. It's a simple yet powerful way to reconnect with your higher self and the vision you're creating.

You can also go a step further by calling the people who gave you those items. Connecting with people who believe in us is needed along our healing journey.

Embracing the Healing Journey

Visualizing your beautiful future is a flowing process that evolves as you do. Embrace the journey! Revisit your vision for the future often, make adjustments as needed, and let it inspire you. With each step, you'll grow closer to the life you've envisioned, and one day you'll look at it and think, "Of course, that's me!"

Keep using the tools that resonate with you the most, keep trusting, and keep moving forward. You are creating something beautiful—and you are worthy of it!

Chapter Eleven

Believe

Nancy is feeling proud of herself for all the work she has put in. Those anxious feelings that she used to experience almost daily are spread out to only a few times a month. When she notices the tightness in her chest and throat, she can slow down and get curious about the triggers, talk to herself with compassion, and process her feelings much easier now. She feels peaceful most of the time. Although she knows there will always be opportunities for growth, she has gratitude for how far she has come. She continues to implement the tools she has learned along the way. Practicing affirmations daily, journaling, and breathwork are helping her decrease her anxiety. On the days when she feels self-doubt creeping in, she works to remind herself about how far she has come.

Her vision board is hanging inside her closet door so she can take a good look at it each morning before she gets dressed. She reminds herself, "I am aligning myself with the future I want and deserve. By knowing how much I desire it, I am embodying my future self and choosing to align my thoughts, my feelings, my behaviors, and the words that come out of my mouth with this vision every day. I am walking the path to bring this amazing vision into my reality."

When you work on visualizing your future, you are getting clarity on what feels intangible. You use your imagination and intuition to bring you closer to your beautiful future. Visualizing may feel abstract, while believing can help you make something that feels unreachable become more tangible. Let's explore how believing is an essential part of connecting and arriving in the future you deserve.

Sometimes it will feel like you don't have all the answers. Belief is about trusting that the answers will reveal themselves from an unexpected source or from within.

Believing in yourself isn't always easy. It will come with some dark days. You will question if you're on the right path, or you'll wonder if you're doing enough to get to the place you want to be in your life. Let me shed some light: You are exactly where you need to be. One day you'll look back at everything you went through, and you're going to see these moments as experiences that helped you develop empathy for others who are where you are now.

Every decision, detour, twist, and turn has brought you right here to this moment. Belief is about leaning into the journey and trusting the path. Sometimes it will feel like you don't have all the answers. Belief is about trusting that the answers will reveal themselves from an unexpected source or from within. Trust your journey, your timing, and your process because your life is unfolding in a way that is uniquely yours.

Another way to believe is to think of it as having faith. Trusting that what is next for you will be ready when you are. It's like driving at night with the headlights on. You can only see so much of the road at a time, and you have to focus on moving forward to see more of it until you find yourself at your destination.

You can't always see what is on its way to you, but it is there, holding you up and gently guiding you forward. For me, having faith is knowing deep down that I am deserving of that amazing future that I desire. It is a whisper in my soul that I must keep going. It is fully trusting without seeing yet.

Maybe for you, it's the way that everything seems to click into place once you stop trying to force things. It could be the way a little sign like lyrics of a song, kind words from a stranger, or a beautiful sunset reminds you to believe in something

> *Believing in your future doesn't have to be big and flashy; it just has to be steady.*

bigger than yourself. Believing in your future doesn't have to be big and flashy; it just has to be steady.

227

Consider the following three steps to strengthen your ability to believe in yourself and the beautiful future you have waiting for you just beyond the horizon. There is no right way to work on these steps. You can revisit them often, and you may need to work on some longer than others to regain your belief. Let's explore them.

Step 1: Consume Wisely

One of the most powerful tools for strengthening your belief is becoming more aware of the content you are feeding your mind, your eyes, and your senses. Are you watching things that motivate you? Do you read or listen to books that inspire you to grow? Are you engaging in conversations that heal and help you believe?

Our need for consumption can change based on external or internal circumstances. Some days, we may not have the emotional capacity to watch something scary. On other days, we may be bored with something silly and light. Neither choice is right or wrong. It just is, so listen to your inner wisdom. The point is consuming wisely and being intentional about what aligns with your best self.

Before COVID-19, I loved watching psychological thrillers and futuristic dystopian movies. They made me feel excited as I tried to figure things out ahead of time, and I loved it when a theory I had turned out to be true. Once COVID-19 happened, they didn't appeal to me as much. I started to notice how stressed they made me feel. When the excitement shifted into feeling a little too close to real life, I stopped watching shows in those genres. I turned my attention to watching series that felt lighter and happier.

Sometimes we watch different things based on what is happening in our lives. When the world around me felt chaotic and scary, I didn't want to watch more of it when I sat down to watch television. Then when life doesn't seem as overwhelming anymore, I'm okay with watching something a little darker. It is about being honest with myself, listening to what feels right in the moment, and following my healing.

When you think about what is happening in your life, do you tend to match that energy with what you choose to watch, or do you look for the opposite of how you're feeling? Take a moment to think about what you're in the mood for the next time you turn on the television, and ask yourself why you're making that choice. Are you letting what you are watching consume you and change your thoughts, feelings, and behaviors? Notice how you feel as you are watching.

Whenever I get ready for work, I can tell that listening to random music puts me in a different mood than when I'm listening to inspirational songs and peaceful, calming music. Knowing that I want to create a peaceful environment for my clients helps me choose music that aligns with harmony and healing.

What you consume has a direct line to your heart, so choose wisely. When you notice your belief in yourself weakening, surround yourself with uplifting voices that can remind you of what's possible for your future. I enjoy consuming inspirational things, like reading or listening to positive affirmations, listening to music that makes me feel connected, or listening to an audiobook that sparks new ideas within me. In those moments that I am getting ready for a talk, I like calling someone who inspires and motivates me. If that is not an option, I provide myself with the most calming and peaceful environment possible. We have the power to engage in things that fill us up, so be mindful of what you consume.

Step 2: Build a Circle That Heals

As humans, we all crave meaningful connection. When we feel disconnected, we struggle. We can feel depressed, lost, or unable to believe in a joyful future. It is important that we find life-giving connections with ourselves and others. Building a circle with healthy connections can motivate us to keep going on our journey to healing from within by helping us feel hopeful and inspired.

Sometimes, when we're exhausted or overwhelmed, it can feel like we lack the emotional or mental capacity to connect with other people. Being around people can feel tedious or draining. That may be a good time to connect with nature instead. You can do some grounding exercises. Go on a walk and connect with trees, or enjoy watching squirrels or birds.

Sometimes we desperately seek external connection, when in reality, what we are missing is connection with ourselves. Take some time to go within and reconnect with yourself. Reading old journals can remind you of where you were at certain points in your life and give you powerful insights about yourself and how far you've come.

Recently, connecting with myself has become a priority. I've noticed the importance of having time by myself to just think and be in my body. I'm working on finding the balance between creating those external connections with other people and having peace internally.

When I push myself to keep reaching out to people and connecting with others without scheduling any alone time, it feels overwhelming and inauthentic. I see myself reaching out just because I feel obligated as opposed to truly being in my heart and flowing with the energy of wanting to hear about the other person. Those inauthentic interactions seem noticeable to me because the conversation is fast-paced and rushed rather than slow, peaceful, and present. In some cases, it can also be noticeable by the other person.

When you are not fully present, you are not honoring yourself because you are not showing up as the best version of yourself. You deserve time to recharge! When you are ready, honor yourself by showing up as your authentic self. That loving, caring, magical person you are. Your light needs to be shared with the world. Doing this will maintain and attract that healing circle you are building.

Honesty and communication will be needed. I had a phone call scheduled with a friend. About half an hour before we were supposed to talk, I sent her a text that I couldn't have the call because I just didn't feel right—I wasn't in the emotional head space to have a loving, best-self conversation with her. We're both into self-development and self-improvement, which can add a level of pressure to our check-in calls. The day I canceled our call, I wasn't in a place to want to discuss new goals, what I'm working on, or what I'm going to improve. Being honest with her felt good because I could let go of the pressure of trying to force a conversation. I honored myself with quiet time instead. I connected with myself first so that I could be ready to engage with her later in a more mindful way.

Another friend of mine and I fell into a routine of hanging out by going out to eat and shopping every time we got together. I explained to her that I wanted to work on some new fitness and financial goals. Going out to expensive restaurants with lots of rich food and then spending money shopping afterward wasn't in alignment with my goals. Walking in the park together would be a new way to connect while helping each other save money and get in some extra steps. When I asked her to change it up by meeting in the park to go on a walk while we talked, she couldn't seem to find the time. We still text each other to check in from time to time, but for right now, we're on different paths.

Building your healing circle will come with evolving friendships. Trust that this is creating space for new healing connections to walk into your life.

For some of us, finding connection with a higher power—God, divine feminine, oneness, or Source—can bring us the peace and clarity we need. It can help us find goodness in the world and belief in humanity, allowing us to show up peacefully as the best versions of ourselves.

I used to be Catholic because it was the religion I was born into. Once I went to college and had some space to consider my spirituality apart from my family, I allowed myself the time to research different religions and paths to see what resonated the most with me. I invite you to explore this area of connection if you feel called to.

As you continue to build meaningful connections to create a circle that heals, remember that you have to be honest and authentic. Show up as your aligned and embodied future self—not just when engaging with others, but when you are by yourself. The most important connection you will ever have is the connection with yourself, so invest time and effort in it.

Step 3: Let Yourself Shine in Your Community

After gaining awareness of what you want to consume and the kinds of connections that are healing, you can continue to grow by sharing your vision with your community. This can create a ripple effect that ends up reaching more people than you could ever imagine. It could heal our world!

Personally, once I have the vision of the future that I'm working toward, I begin to ask myself, "How am I showing up? How am I using what I am learning to improve my community? How can I create a bigger impact toward the healing of our world?"

It is about staying aligned with the vision of my future self and believing it is possible to make a difference even though it can be scary or uncomfortable at times.

To be honest, I know some days we can't see past our present issue. When you encounter those days, it is okay to pause until you are in the right mindset or headspace. When I have those moments, I can go back to the other steps of believing. If I don't feel ready to jump into action with step 3, I can go back to step 2 and check in on my connection with myself. I can also go to step 1 and think about the feelings that come along with the books I'm reading or the music I'm listening to. I recently created an "Inspiration and Connection" list on my planner that includes videos and songs that make me feel connected to my purpose and bring me back to belief and alignment.

When you work through these steps, discomfort is a given because you are trying something new. You are learning to choose yourself, and you're stepping into a new version of yourself. So remember, there is no growth without discomfort.

If we have experienced a lot of trauma, our discomfort tolerance can be a bit smaller, causing us to back up at the earliest sign of feeling out of our comfort zone. It's important to really tune in with ourselves and be honest.

Are we challenging ourselves and growing through those uncomfortable feelings?

We have to find a balance where we can push ourselves without setting ourselves up to get overwhelmed to the point where we back up and never try again. Show up aligned, not perfect. Meet yourself where you are, and make sure you're growing with a healthy amount of discomfort.

I used to be in Toastmasters International for public speaking, where I met someone who told me I should reach out to our local news or morning shows to offer insight to current events from a therapist's perspective. I looked into it and sent a couple of emails. When I didn't hear back from them, I created a story in my mind about why they didn't get back to me, and I let that story stop me from trying again.

The good news is that while writing this chapter, I decided to reach out to those news channels again! I decided to believe in myself and ask, "What if the best-case scenario happens?" By doing this, I have the potential to make a bigger impact in my community.

As you may have noticed by now, I have struggled with this feeling that I don't belong and that I have to be more or do more. It's like a quiet pressure to constantly perform, to earn my place, to do enough. It is something I continue to work on even now.

In 2019, I got invited to a women's networking group in a wealthy suburb near me. Walking in, I felt uncomfortable. Most of the women were tall, blond, and fit. In my eyes, they exemplified wealth and confidence. This made me feel like an outsider who didn't belong.

I kept driving to those meetings in my older Cadillac. Even though I felt like I didn't fit in, I kept going and showing up as my best self. Before leaving my house, I would do some grounding exercises and breathing techniques. On the drive to the meeting, I would listen to inspirational music and say affirmations like, "I belong. I am beautiful. I am confident." I made sure I kept talking to people, introducing myself, and talking about my business.

For about a year, I made it to those weekly meetings even though about 80 percent of the time, I felt like I didn't belong. During that time, I became very confident when it came to speaking about my counseling business because I was discussing it so frequently.

I began getting invited to work in other school districts as a result of the weekly networking meetings. I got to speak about my process and inspire students during three different open-table interview sessions. I got to help students believe in their dreams by speaking about what it was like for me to go to college and start my own business. I know if I hadn't pushed through those feelings of not fitting in, I wouldn't have had those opportunities to branch out to school districts in communities that were about an hour away from my office.

It wasn't easy, but my perseverance paid off in the end. Letting yourself shine in your community can influence and make an impact in others believing in the possibilities. That is the magic of being grounded and connected to your best self as you push through the discomfort—believing that by putting in the work, more blessings will come.

You Belong in the Life You Imagine

Believe that your vision is possible, and keep working on it consistently and from a place of love. Even if someone who hears your vision chooses to share their opinion on how unrealistic or impossible it sounds. Sharing your vision with a friend or acquaintance doesn't mean you are asking them for permission to go after what you want in life.

Remember that someone else's opinion about your future doesn't get to shake up your belief and override what aligns with where you want to be. Typically, when someone gives their opinion, you can think of them telling you to put on a jacket because it's cold outside. They may want to be helpful, but don't listen if it isn't something you align with as you may not need their help in that way.

This happened when I shared my goal of opening my own counseling private practice with an old friend. She told me about how hard it would be to get clients, that I wouldn't know how much money I would be able to make from one month to the next, and that she'd much rather stay working at an agency where she didn't have to worry about all those other things. I realized that although she thought she was helping me, I didn't need to hear all her reasons why I should doubt the vision that was aligned with my life.

I chose to distance myself because I knew I didn't need to continuously consume her concerns when she didn't share my vision. At the time, I was not ready to have an assertive conversation. Looking back, I could have chosen to share my concerns and then identify if the friendship was worth keeping. You belong in the life you imagine, so don't let anyone tell you otherwise.

At a workshop I attended, we looked at our inner circle and closest friends and how we interact with one another. I realized that I like to be the motivator. I love to be the friend who inspires and empowers others. It feels great to be seen as an expert in my field. I also noticed that I felt uncomfortable with people who were more accomplished than me. The feelings of not belonging were still resurfacing. I'm still working on the times I get triggered and start comparing myself, having to process those automatic feelings of not being enough. I redirect myself and use the tools in this book to center myself. Stopping myself from talking to people who have accomplished more than me is a way of selling myself short. But now that I have created the awareness, I can choose differently. I know that I am aligned and I am worthy of the life I am creating.

Selling ourselves short usually comes from doubt, fear, lack, and scarcity mindsets. It can be caused by years of trauma and feeling like a victim. As you continue to grow through this, know that interacting with someone you look up to can amplify your progress and cause you to continue to move forward in powerful ways. Be honest with yourself about how many people you allow to speak into your life who are living in that comfort zone, because they don't help you move forward. Work on finding the right balance between friends you motivate and inspire and friends who do the same for you because they are already where you want to be.

Even though it can be uncomfortable, having those friends or acquaintances who feel like your heroes or people who are already where you want to be can help you get to the next level. Seeing them achieving their goals can motivate and inspire you to take the steps to get to the next level.

Be mindful of the comparison trap. There is a difference between seeking out others who inspire you and looking at them in a way that makes you doubt yourself and your ability to bring your vision of the future to life. My mindset is that these friends have already reached a level of success for them, and although I want the same for myself, I can hold space and be happy for them at the same time. The fact that they have already accomplished these goals provides a window for me to see the possibility that I can have it too. Let's believe that being in the same environment as them makes it easier for us to make it happen too.

Go into relationships with people you admire with a healthy mindset of being open to new possibilities rather than seeing where they are and what they have as an area of lack for yourself. Chances are, their success didn't happen overnight, so give yourself some grace and have a conversation with them about what it was like when they were where you are right now. It will be an amazing eye-opening experience for you.

Keep Going—You Are Worth It

Life can feel like a roller coaster sometimes. We won't get to a point where we say, "Okay, I did all this work, and now I'm done. I'm all healed up, and everything will be perfect from this moment forward."

We will all have days when we feel like we're on top of the world and others when we have to face setbacks. Remember that this is part of the journey. What is different is that you now have tools to help you focus, trust, and believe that the sunrise is coming again tomorrow.

As I was working on this chapter, I decided to look through some old notes on my bookshelf because I was feeling pretty productive. Then my bookshelf collapsed, and everything fell on the floor. Instead of immediately cleaning everything up, I decided to take a break. I allowed myself some time to feel sad about this bookcase I've had for years. I paused to release my feelings and decided to take a break and feel cheerful by watching one episode of a show.

When the show ended, I took the next small, actionable step—going online to find a new bookcase. Once that problem was solved, I continued working without feeling like I was forcing myself and just pushing my feelings down. This was a tiny setback, but we are going to encounter various ones along the way. Welcome them because they are helping you grow.

When you are working toward your goal and some unforeseen setback pops up, it's okay to cry if you need to, and allow yourself to feel whatever it is you're feeling. Release the feeling of sadness or frustration and forgive yourself. Process and keep going. This is something you are continuously going to work on, and you are doing your best. Focus on your vision, and remind yourself that the amazing future you desire is coming.

Continue working through the three steps of belief, because your wonderful future is closer than you think. Keep taking the next small step that feels right. I believe in you!

Chapter Twelve

Receive

Gaby used to define herself as a habitual giver. Throughout her journey, she has realized the importance of allowing the space to let others give back to her. Receiving the gift of time alone to recharge at the retreat from her mom and husband opened her eyes to a life that allowed her to put herself first.

Since then, she has been working on creating boundaries that reflect her new understanding that to have the future she deserves, she needs to pour into herself first. When she takes time to take care of herself and relax, she can show up as her best self and give to others more authentically.

Gaby still has moments when she feels guilty for turning down the opportunity to host an event in her home. But watching other church members light up at the chance to host helps her to see that other people are willing to be more involved if she gives them the opportunity. On those days, she has time to bake something to take to someone else's house without feeling the extra pressure of hosting. Her family notices how calm and happy she is as they ride in the car together, singing along to the radio on the way to the next fellowship event.

She still has moments when it's easier to give than to receive. She reminds herself to say "Thank you" and accept her friend's compliment on her skirt instead of brushing it away.

She appreciates her husband trying to show more affection and romanticism, and she lets him know she is grateful for the flowers he brings her. Knowing that his love language is physical touch, she lets their hugs linger and finds ways to express her love for him by holding his hand and snuggling with him on the couch for movie nights.

Gaby's transformation isn't perfect. She has come to understand that she feels better—mentally, physically, and spiritually—the more she becomes in tune with the ebb and flow of giving and receiving.

The Healing Flow

There is a natural flow that comes with giving and receiving as you work toward creating the future of your dreams. Your intention and energy speak, and they matter as much as the behavior you engage in. Nature is aware of the constant flow of giving and receiving. Consider the trees. They have to receive water and carbon dioxide if they're going to give us oxygen. Then we take in oxygen and exhale carbon dioxide. In the natural world, we rely on both sides of this flow to survive. It is similar to giving and receiving. If we get stuck on the giving side of things, we can wear ourselves out and create resentment toward the person who is great at

> *Your intention and energy speak, and they matter as much as the behavior you engage in.*

receiving but not giving. Think of Gaby and how she became depressed because she forgot about herself.

A balance is necessary to maintain our humanity and live our dream life. Pay attention to the energy in the flow of giving and receiving in your daily life. If you are just giving and giving like Gaby used to, you become uncomfortable when it comes time to receive. If you are only receiving, you are at risk of becoming a taker, and people may decide to distance themselves from you because you may seem incapable of giving.

If you are too much of one side, it can be uncomfortable for you and the people around you. Work on creating a balance in this constant flow of giving and receiving that resonates with you.

My younger brother is naturally a giver. Anytime I'm frustrated or need to talk something through, he is my go-to person to call for wise words and comfort. He guides me and holds space for me to process my worries. I love connecting with him, but when I struggle with self-worth or feeling like I'm not good enough, I start to feel like I need to give something back to him. This is when I try to overcompensate and bombard him with questions, "How are you doing? Do you need anything from me? What do you need? How can I help?"

But I'm learning that letting him take care of me during those times is actually giving him a sense of purpose by allowing him to help me.

In 2024, my husband and I decided to work together on our relationship. What came out from that time was my struggle with receiving. I am very aware that my husband supports me and is there for me. I know I can trust him, and he wants to be a provider in our relationship. But my struggle with receiving can sometimes lead to self-sabotaging and then creating arguments because I want to lead.

I've realized that I was afraid with thoughts like, *What if everything does work out? What if he's the love of my life and we have this amazing relationship, and then I lose him?*

Those kinds of thoughts used to feel scary to me because a part of me felt like I would save myself from the pain of losing him if I kept myself closed off. I wasn't sure I could allow myself to receive his unconditional love so fully.

But I've learned that by limiting the amount of love I share with him, I'm actually causing myself more pain in the long run. If I continue to stay closed off and lose him one day, the pain is going to come—not just from the natural grieving process, but also from guilt and self-hatred for not allowing our relationship to experience my loving, authentic self. So instead of denying myself of an incredible relationship out of the fear of losing it, I'm working on being more present and letting myself flow as we give and receive each other's love.

Establishing my practice and putting in the time to expand and network with others used to feel like solely my responsibility. The beliefs I brought with me from growing up with a single mom made it easy for me to think that I had to make it on my own. I used to be of the mindset that if I'm going to create all these things and you want to come along, great! If not, I'll keep going without you, and you can step aside while I continue forward. But I have realized that I can allow myself to receive and work together with my team and we can all win.

Receiving my husband's help with the counseling practice involves a lot of internal work on my part. I use affirmations like *I am able to receive, It is easy for me to receive,* and *I can lean into my feminine energy of receiving.*

Having those thoughts in my mind helps me to see him as a partner who is there to help support me instead of a threat coming in to take over. It's an everyday intention that we're in this together. I can receive his help by delegating tasks and allowing him to take ownership, knowing that we are a team and partners in life and business.

To be honest, it was a struggle at first. I remember thinking, *Why are you saying "our" business? This is* my *business.*

I've realized that thinking in that manner was coming from fear and lack as opposed to a place of abundance and limitlessness. After shifting my mindset and allowing myself to be part of a team, it gets easier to see that we created it together. He invested in it, and I put in the work to make it what it has become. It's like our baby. It belongs to both of us, and we want to work together to see it continue to thrive.

Earlier in our partnership, I used to tell him that my role was CEO and he was more of a manager. I would agree to hear him, but at the end of the day, I was making my own decisions. As an older sibling, there is a tendency to want to be in charge.

Now I feel like I receive his opinion more easily when I focus on listening to him from a place of love and understanding. I'm not afraid to ask him what he thinks of different possible new hires. I understand the kind of person he likes hiring. I can tell whether a person will be a good fit for him just during the phone screening with a candidate, and I can make the decision not to move forward to an interview. We continue to work together on keeping the flow of giving and receiving as we grow together in our businesses.

During the transition of my husband having more ownership and decision-making in the practice, we didn't agree on a potential new hire. I had a feeling that she wasn't going to be a good fit, but my husband thought she would make a great addition to the team. I reluctantly hired her, and she and I began going through the training portion of her onboarding process. Training her never felt quite right, and I had a massive headache for three days straight while I tried to push through and get her ready.

My outward behavior was there: I was kind to her, tried to be present and take things slowly, modeled how we do things, and answered all her questions. Internally, I felt like I was just going through the motions; it was a struggle.

After a month, she decided she couldn't handle the job, and she quit. I learned that if my body is speaking to me and I know from the start that someone won't be a good fit, it's better to listen than to engage and feel drained and inauthentic while trying to make something work. It is about finding the balance of giving and receiving while also listening to my body.

Now my husband and I communicate our concerns and what our intuitions are telling us about different candidates. We have learned to take things slow and trust that the right team members are coming.

Your body is communicating with you all the time. I invite you to look at your life and find the relationships that drain you. If you notice that you're trying to push yourself along in an unhealthy relationship or friendship, it's okay to take a step back and give yourself time to consider your options. If you continue on this path, you are limiting yourself from the flow of giving and receiving. You are staying stuck and limiting the space for amazing friendships. It can lead to more misalignment and internal struggle, potentially causing you to feel unhappy and unsupported by the people around you.

We all deserve happy and healthy relationships.

We all deserve happy and healthy relationships. I'm continuing to learn how to navigate our business decisions with the intention of the future I see for us. I want to be in a healthy relationship. I want us to be able to communicate and talk about the difficulties we face and be truly partners in the business and our personal lives. When I feel stressed about something at work, I can express safely to let him know that I'm not ready to talk about it yet. I can give us time to process what happened, and then we can give ourselves some time later to come back together and have a productive conversation. It is about taking responsibility for how I am showing up in our relationship.

When I catch myself struggling to receive, I like to visualize myself as a beautiful flower that is open and ready for positive energy, love, and abundance. I make sure that I receive everything that aligns with me and my future, and I release anything that doesn't serve me. It is about being at ease with the flow of giving and receiving. When I give, I like to focus on sending good intentions and peace with anyone I help. I visualize white and gold rays being sent out from my body. What visual can you use to help you tune in into being open to give and receive?

As you open yourself up to being able to receive your beautiful future, incorporate the following tools to create a flowing relationship with giving and receiving.

Service with Compassion

Serving others is part of the constant flow of giving and receiving. We are all one, and many times, what one person needs is something that we all can benefit from. Think about the reasons why you are working on healing yourself. Yes, it is to feel better, to receive the life you want, and to get the peace you have been searching for. But it is also to give your best self to the people you care about and to support your loved ones.

Maybe you want to improve your relationships or maybe you want to uplift your children, parents, spouse, or neighbors. Being of service from a place of compassion is part of the healing journey. As you are in the flow of being of service to others, this energy is just going to expand. It starts with you and then radiates out.

I work on growing my business not just because I want financial stability but also because I want to make a bigger impact and help more people heal. I take my mission seriously and want to help others on this path, because as I do that, I continue to heal myself. That is the magic of serving with compassion—it creates the natural flow of giving and receiving.

It's important to realize that when you are helping other people, you are also helping yourself grow and learn right along with them. In sessions (or even as I worked through the process of writing this book), I get reminders of all the skills to practice and which ones I still need to work on.

Helping others keeps you in a constant state of flow. Think of serving with compassion as giving from a place of abundance—pouring into yourself first and then being ready to pour into someone else. As you focus outward on other people, things are happening to you. It can vary from person to person, but when you are struggling internally, being able to help somebody else can give you that inspiration and motivation to keep going.

Serving others is something that my mom instilled in me from a young age. As a Catholic single mom, she has always been a giver. Her goal was to teach me that we need to love our neighbors as we love ourselves. She seemed to interpret that verse as loving her neighbors more than herself. She found ways for me to volunteer as a young girl. I remember her encouraging me to talk to the people in a nursing home. Another time, she took me to a company that only hired people with physical and developmental disabilities. I sat with them and talked with them while they worked. She wanted me to have experience helping others no matter their background or current situation.

The experiences that my mom gave me to interact with people different from me contributed to the empathy I have as an adult. As a teenager, I saw how my peers looked down on people who were different from them, thinking they were stupid or gross in some way. Because of the experiences I had, I developed the awareness that we're all people with feelings and we don't always know what someone else is going through.

It reminds me of a paper I wrote in college with a visual of someone driving an old, beat-up car and people judging them, thinking they don't know how to manage their finances or they're poor. But what if driving that old car is an amazing accomplishment for that person?

The truth is that we don't know people's stories, and keeping our mind open with curiosity and our heart open with empathy can create a wonderful experience of giving and receiving. We can always learn from others, no matter their stories or current circumstances.

When you take the time to develop empathy and truly understand someone else, you cannot only serve them better but also receive what they have to offer. And sometimes this receiving doesn't come from the person you gave to.

Be open to the possibilities. Trust that what you want is coming to you, and it may come from an unexpected source. Knowing how good it makes someone feel when you help them makes it easier to get into the flow of giving and receiving authentically. Empathy is not about giving to receive, but about giving from the heart and sharing our gifts.

With empathy, you can experience joy right along with the people you serve in big and small ways.

You Deserve Joy

As you continue on this healing journey, remember to celebrate your progress no matter how small. This could be anything from planning a trip once a year to daily self-talk that is encouraging. Maybe you look in the mirror after you brush your teeth at night and tell yourself something like, "I'm amazing. I did this. I'm such an incredible mom, teacher, and friend."

It could also be taking two weeks of vacation to travel to a place you've never been as a reward for working so hard all year. Maybe you take a month to go stay with your brother and help him with his kids. Give yourself the opportunity to celebrate and experience joy along your healing journey.

Your future isn't just about constantly doing the work, developing yourself, and improving. It's also about taking a pause to see how far you've come and enjoying your progress. Take time to celebrate how you talk to yourself, your healthy everyday thoughts, and the big things as frequently as possible—once per quarter, twice per year, or even once a year for those big celebrations.

Make sure that you connect back with the people you care about and with your inner child. Maybe you loved dancing as a child, so you sign up for a dance camp to help you connect back to that happiness and fun.

Celebrating keeps you on the constant flow of giving and receiving because you are giving yourself freedom, peace, and happiness. As you're taking care of yourself, your joy can be contagious to those around you.

Imagine the possibilities if we all lived from this place of joy. We would be able to give to the people in your community from a place of self-love, empathy, and compassion. We would look beyond ourselves to find individuals and organizations that we could support. This would create a ripple effect that could expand far beyond our wildest dreams.

During the first year of my practice, I had a hard time turning work off and stopping. I was always looking for ways to grow the business faster, improve the website, and network with more people to make them aware of my services. I used to be up working on my computer until midnight or one in the morning without realizing that I was on the path to burn out.

I began implementing things like telling myself ten o'clock was the absolute latest time to shut down my computer. It was stressful. I sat there staring at the closed laptop wondering what I should do with my time. I felt like Gaby, binge-watching television and trying to relax and just feeling like I was wasting my time.

But it got better when I understood that attaching myself to my career kept me from other parts of myself that I was neglecting. I had to learn that I deserve rest. I also allowed myself to experience joy and fun.

I bought some coloring books and started journaling. I connected with my inner child and got Zumba certified. I took singing lessons and even golf lessons. Trying so many different things comes from the very high expectations my mom had for us.

Monday through Friday, we went to school and then participated in after-school activities. Saturdays were for cleaning—the house, the bedding, the laundry—then folding and putting the laundry away. On Sundays, we woke up early, went to church, got something to eat, and then prepared for the week. That meant packing lunches, setting out our uniforms, and cleaning our shoes so they were ready for school.

Resting was not something that we practiced. The only time our mom modeled resting was when she was forced into her bed when she got sick with the flu about once per year. So I had years of practice in exerting myself. I had to relearn to rest and take a break.

I started setting boundaries with my colleagues, beginning with letting them know they could email me with questions or concerns outside of work hours that weren't emergencies. I spent the first seven years creating systems and figuring out by trial and error what worked and what didn't. This required a mindset shift: "I am not a victim, and

I don't have to be a martyr. I can have a successful business that feels light and in flow."

Now I know that taking time to celebrate is a conscious decision I need to make: I am learning that what I do is enough.

Last year, I took three weeks off in December and decided to no longer plan anything on Sundays. Every Saturday night, I feel like a little kid the night before a day off of school. I wake up early, excited about the possibilities that a free day brings. Sundays are designated for weekly celebrations and rest, and they're always a lot of fun. Whether it's hanging out with a friend, cleaning the house, going to the park, going through the car wash—whatever I want to do!

You deserve joy! Consider ways that you would like to celebrate your progress as you move closer to the future you envisioned.

Be the Hope You Seek

As our time together comes to an end, I want to remind you to keep your hope alive. Hope is something we can draw from those around us—those who inspire us, motivate us, and share their wisdom when we need it the most. There will be times when even the words of others won't feel like enough. In those moments, you can choose to give hope to yourself. My brother once told me that even on the darkest days, you can find a speck of light within you.

Look back on your own story. Remember your past successes, the moments when you worked hard, persevered, and achieved your goals. Think about how much resilience and strength you've shown over the years. You've faced challenges, and yet here you are, still moving forward, growing into the incredible person you're becoming. Let those reminders light your way when the path feels dark. Healing is within you.

Hope is also about recognizing your humanity and your potential. You are worthy of hope, joy, and all the good things life has to offer just because you are alive. You don't need to earn it; it's yours simply because you exist. When doubts start to creep in, remind yourself that you are part of something bigger. You are connected to God, Source, and the infinite energy that flows through every living being. That connection is your proof that hope belongs to you, always.

Hope tells us that what we see in others is a reflection of what's already within us, waiting to bloom.

When you see others thriving—whether it's in love, success, or joy—know that it's not out of reach for you. Their achievements are a reminder of what's possible for you. If they have those things, so can you! Hope tells us that what we see in others is a reflection of what's already within us, waiting to bloom.

As you close this book and step back into the world, carry hope with you. Tune in to what you've accomplished, the oneness you share with God and humanity, and the infinite possibilities ahead. Hope isn't just something you have—it's something you are. With it, you can create a life filled with all the good things you deserve. You got this!

My Love Letter to You

T hank you for opening your heart.

Thank you for reading these words, for letting them move through you, and for allowing yourself to feel, process, and release. I am so proud of you for choosing yourself—your healing, your truth, your wholeness, and the future that has always been waiting for you. I celebrate you for putting in the work.

This book is more than a collection of tools and stories. It's a piece of my own healing that I've gently placed in your hands. Now it lives inside of you too, woven into your own becoming. I hope it met you with compassion, care, and enough light to carry you forward when the road felt unclear.

Your healing journey won't always be easy, but it will be worth it. With every step, you are returning to your most radiant self. The version of you that is not only possible, but inevitable: the version of you that was never broken, only buried under the weight of what you've survived.

Please know that I am with you, now and always. In the quiet moments, the celebrations, and the chapters that still feel tender and unfinished. I am wrapping you in white and gold rays of light and sending you the kind of healing energy that lingers and lifts. Even when it's hard, when you feel like giving up, and when you wonder if you've lost your way, I want you to know that you are not alone.

You are filled with so much light. Trust that it is there, and let this be your reminder:

- You are enough.
- You are not too late.
- You do not have to prove anything to anyone else.
- You are worthy of rest, joy, softness, and love.
- You are worthy of every single thing you desire.

Keep being brave—not by pushing harder, but by pausing, breathing, and being present. Keep believing in the magic that rises when you trust yourself. Keep reaching toward the life that is already reaching back for you. When the day feels heavy or your heart needs a reminder, come back to this book. Let it hold you, whisper hope when you forget, and remind you how far you've already come.

Thank you for trusting me with your heart and letting me walk beside you. I hope every page reminded you of your own brilliance, power, tenderness, and magic. I believe in you with the certainty that the sun will rise again. Fully. Unconditionally. Forever.

With all the love I have,

Carla

Acknowledgments

Thank you to all who made this book possible. You inspire me more than you know, and I will always be grateful.

Gracias a mi madre, Mirta Zúñiga, por creer en mi y por mostrarme que el amor incondicional existe. Admiro tu fortaleza. Gracias por ser mi madre y darme todo lo que necesito para crecer en esta vida.

To my husband, David Niño, for allowing me the space to continue healing by making me feel safe. Your quiet and steady support has carried me farther than you know. I admire your commitment.

To my students at Casey Elementary, for opening your hearts to me and believing in me. You are capable of magic and limitless love. I will forever cherish the years we spent together. I hope our paths cross again.

To Lewis Howes, without you this book wouldn't exist. Your unwavering commitment to helping others is inspiring. Thank you for being a light in the world.

To StoryBuilders, especially Tracy Jenkins, Andrew Biernat, and Bill Blankschaen. Thank you for your support and for helping me bring this book into existence. You guys are amazing, and I am blessed I got to write this book with you.

To my clients, for being brave, for believing in me, and for doing the work to continue to heal. I am so proud of you!

May you continue healing and creating ripples of peace everywhere you go.

To you, the reader, thank you! Thank you for choosing this book and walking this path with me. Continue saying yes to your healing because your story matters more than you know. May you continue embodying the best version of yourself.

Gracias a mi padre, Carlos Calderas, por trabajar en nuestra relación y por mostrarme que nunca es tarde para reparar. Gracias por ayudarme a sanar.

With all my heart,

Carla